Mitch Kemmer

As the Son of a Dog Man ... I Became a Hog Hunter
by Mitch Kemmer

ISBN: 978-1-7328283-1-5

Printed in the United States

CONTENTS

Preface

This book is one in a series of books on Norman Kemmer and his life with the American Pit Bull Terrier. Wild Boar Hunting was one of his passions concerning these dogs. Hog Hunting would take him from his first Pit Bulldog to his grave. I was lucky enough to have been his son, and feel that his story is worth sharing. This story is what is referred to as a Historical Fiction. It will contain stories of crossing State lines illegally, Hunting in 'no hunting' areas, transporting hogs from State to State, and other illegal affairs, to say the least. If this were an actual accurate history then that would make me a criminal, and I would never knowingly break the law. This is a story based on the life of a man who loved his dogs, and loved to hunt wild hogs, but as in all Historical Fictions many of the names, places, and events may have been changed.

Chapter 1
WILD BOAR HUNTING IS A SPORT OF KINGS

The hunting of Wild Boar is a time honored tradition among Royalty, Military Men, the Aristocracy, and the common every day Big Game Trophy Hunter. In the United States today the hunting of Wild Boar has become the second most popular Big Game Animal to be hunted, second only to Whitetail Deer. In Europe it is still a time honored tradition in many countries. But in recent years the Wild Boar, due to modern TV propaganda, is being viewed as a nuisance more so than a respected trophy animal. Thanks to my father Norman Kemmer I became a Wild Boar hunter at a young age and developed the same respect for his toughness and the challenge he presents, that Kings and Royalty of old had for him. We are here to take a look at his history, which is as old as mankind himself, and the way he was viewed in the past. Also the challenges and adventures that he afforded me and my father. Then we will take a look at where he ranks, and should rank, in modern hunting societies.

The famous Greek Historian Homer wrote about Wild Boar Hunting as being the single hunt that provided the most honor and challenge. He wrote of it being a hunt for Kings, soldiers, and in many cases a hunt that provided young men with the challenges that provided them with a passage into proving their manhood. Homer wrote these things Centuries before the birth of Christ. Hercules, the Greek God, was said to be a Wild Boar Hunter.

The English Mythological figure, King Arthur, was also said to have been an avid Wild Boar Hunter. Think of it this way. King Arthur was a myth designed to show all the aspects of the finest man that could be imagined. Honor, code, loyalty, etc. He is held up to Kings and subjects throughout England and the world as the example of what a man should be and how he should conduct himself. Then we see that his favorite sport of hunting to test his courage and his skills with a blade, is to hunt Wild Boar.

Wild Boar hunting has often been a way for soldiers world wide to test and hone there skills for combat. Warriors would often hunt from horse back, but upon approaching the Wild Boar would dismount to face him head on. This was to test their courage and to work on there skills either with a knife or a spear. Soldiers in India, known as lancers, often did their Wild Boar hunts from horse back to test their abilities against a prey that would give them the closest challenge that they would have to a real man to man combat threat. These hunts to prepare these men for combat showed the constant respect that men of honor and Royalty have always viewed the Wild Boar as the most challenging of hunts. The Boar's ability to slash, stab, and even kill at times has put them on the world stage as one of the toughest and most dangerous of game. They have always been in the places where they live, viewed much like the Cape Buffalo of the African Continent. In the country of India, it was often said by the old timers that Wild Boar could be seen at a watering hole drinking between two Tigers. It has also been said for hundreds of years that many times Mature Wild Boars have been recorded to have killed Tigers.

(Above) Floor mosaic, 4th century, from a Roman villa near Merida, Spain. (Below) Picksticking from horseback in India.

One of the single most famous of all the Royal paintings comes from the artist Diego Velazquez in around 1635. It is a painting of the French King Philip IV on a Wild Boar Hunt. The paintings fame is due to the fact that Philip IV died as a result of that Wild Boar Hunt. During the hunt a Boar charged King Philip as he was approaching him on horseback. As Philip fell from the horse his aides around him rushed to his aide, but he died as a result of the fall. It would be difficult to find another Big Game Animal, other than on the continent of Africa, that would charge a group of 15 or so men mounted on horseback. Most would flee in that situation, and it would be a chase, instead of a fight. This is why men of Royalty and Military Men had such a deep respect for this animal. This death of King Philip IV was tragic but he did not choose to play golf, he chose to be a Wild Boar Hunter. He chose an adversary worthy of a King.

Diego Velazquez's famous painting of King Philip IV wild boar hunt, which resulted in his death.

King Richard III of England, who was famous for his death in the War of the Roses in 1485 at the Battle of Bosworth Field, used a 'White Boar' as his personal device, or badge. King Edward III had used a Blue Boar, but his descendant King Richard III chose a White Boar to represent him. He gave replicas of a White Boar out to all of his nobles that served him loyally. One was discovered in the tomb of Sir Ralph Fitzherbert who served Richard III, and died in 1483. These medals, if you will, seemed to be awarded for bravery in battle. This would be the equivalent of Germany's Iron Cross, or the United States Congressional Medal of Honor. In recent years a search for the actual site of King Richard III's death has been ongoing. Archaeologist Dr. Glenn Ford recently found in 2009 a silver gift witch may have unearthed the secret of the site. A White Boar Medallion made of pure silver was found near the site of a small Medieval Marsh. Historians know that the King was killed when his horse became stuck in a mire during the final charge of the Battle of Bosworth Field. This White Boar Medal that was retrieved was made of pure silver. In the old days the more precious the metal that a gift was made of, the more important the recipient of it. Historians believe that this White Boar Medal being made of pure silver would have meant that it was given in honor to one of Richard's own Knights. On the day of this final charge the King was known to have had several Knights that rode with him to his death in battle. What an honor to have died in battle. Many historians said that Richard had every chance to retreat, knowing that the battle was lost, but instead chose a death with honor. He chose to meet that death in a head on charge into forces that greatly outnumbered him. It sounds like King Richard III of England chose to

King Richard III's white boar badge found in the tomb of Sir Ralph Fitzherbert who died in 1483

take his death in the same fashion that the outnumbered Wild Boar in the famous hunt with France's King Philip IV, chose to take his death. Outnumbered and with no chance that Boar chose to charge King Phillip IV and his group of assistants, all mounted on horses, head on. What a fine death. Perhaps that is why King Richard III chose the Boar as the symbol of his Royal House. Rewarding his brave knights with medals carved in the symbol of the bravest Big Game Animal on their continent.

Richard and his son standing on boars in a contemporary heraldic roll.

Over and over again throughout the ages this animal has been worshiped and respected for his bravery in the face of death. The ancient Celts considered the Wild Boar to be their most sacred animal. Freyr, the Norse God of Fertility was said to have had a magical boar named Gullinbursti. In the labour's of Herakles, his third one was to capture a Erymanthian Boar. Adonis was said to have been killed by a Wild Boar. It was said that Odysseus, who often traveled in disguise, was always easily recognizable due to many scars he carried from hunting Wild Boar as a young man. Over and over again throughout history from the beginning of mankind, we find references to the Wild Boar as to his ferocity and the respect he was given as a challenge to his hunter.

(Above) Freyr, the Norse God of Fertility, with his Magical Boar Gullinbursti.

(Below) A statue of Herakles with the Erymanthian Boar.

Perhaps the greatest respect given to the Wild Boar from the middle ages until today was the design of the weapons used against him. Hunters world wide have always hunted with Spears. The design of the spear is very simple, a long shaft with a pointed tip. Spears designed for hunting Boar had a 'Crosspiece' situated at the end of the spear tip. Usually about 18 or so inches back on the spear from the very tip. This crosspiece design on spears made especially for Boars were never used on spears for any other kind of hunting, nor for warfare. This crosspiece was there for a simple reason. It was to stop the Boar from running back up the spear shaft and killing the man holding the spear. With Deer, Bear, and even Lion hunting in Africa, the spear design did not have this crosspiece because after being speared the game usually ran away and died. Wild Boar on the other hand would charge his enemy and impale his own body on to the spear to reach his enemy. It was said that even a crucial stab into the heart would not stop a Boar's charge, and without the stop he would have time to severely injure or kill his enemy before he bled out. The crosspiece would serve to stop this and therefore allow the man with the spear to hold the Boar off of him until he died. Again, this simple design alone, found only on Spears that were special made for Boar Hunting, shows how much respect was paid to this fierce Big Game Animal. One of the most famous modern day spear makers is a company called 'Cold Steel'. They have many spear designs, but the one they call 'The Boar Spear' has this crosspiece. I saw a good friend of mine named Doug Hahn spear a charging Boar with the Cold Steel Boar Spear. Doug made a deadly stick on the Boar and as he charged, the crosspiece stopped the boar from running the spear all the way through him. The impact knocked Doug down and he was able to keep the Boar off of him only due to the crosspiece. As Doug fell back the end of the spear hit the ground and the Boar, charging forward, was picked up about 3 feet off the ground and almost went completely over his fallen enemy. Doug owed a lot to this crosspiece design that stretches back to Medieval times. Prior to this design many hunters were reported to have been killed by Boar even as the animal was dying. What a fine adversary.

A Medieval Boar Hunt. Notice the Cross Piece on the Spear.

The respect shown to the Boar above all other animals in this time frame is evident in so many ways related to Kings, Knights, Barons, and all military men. His fierceness in battle when facing his own death was the reason for this respect. Soldiers all hoped to be as brave when faced with death as he was. Another sign of their respect for him was that many military men had symbols of the Wild Boar on their helmets, clothes, and flags. The mighty Beowulf was said to have had images of Boar on his helmet. Persian soldiers from the old days adorned themselves in military clothing with Wild Boar on them as they did their Boar hunting from the backs of their War Elephants. Many of the poems from the old days talked of a Wild Boar's toughness and willingness to welcome combat, insisting that Wild Boar could always be heard sharpening their teeth as they welcomed their enemies approach. Soldiers loved the Boar hunt because it's challenges in close quarter danger checked not only their nerve, but their skills with a blade. Other forms of hunting involved the animals fleeing, and only tested the soldier's skill with arrows or the throwing of a spear at animal in flight. The courageous Boar provided a hunt for a real man wanting to test himself.

Hunting the Wild Boar with dogs was always the preferred method. In old historical studies of battle armor, one can find that in the 16th and 17th centuries they even began fitting armor for there dogs that they hunted Boar with. In this same time frame can also be found the fitting of armor for the hunter with facing Wild Boar down. Along with the crosspiece on the Spears designed for Boar hunting, they also began in the 16th century to put similar cross pieces on swords made specially for the pursuit of Boar. The Sword allowed the hunter to get even closer than the Spear which would put even more of the hunters courage on display. Hunters would brag on scars from their Boar hunts in close quarters, but wanted the cross piece on their swords to potentially save their lives. All in all the Boar was by far the most preferred of wild game to test a man's metal. Anglo Saxon men throughout this time period named many of their sons after the Wild boar. Any discussion of Boar hunting in written history always spoke of the 'Thrilling Danger' of the hunt. Death's of Princes and Nobleman during Wild Boar hunts were constantly being recorded such as the West Frankish King Carloman II in 884, Hungarian Prince Imre in 1031, and Edward de Vere, Earl of Oxford in 1392.

The first recorded hunting preserve for Wild Boar was done by the Roman Fulvius Lippinus. His hunting area was on his land in Tarquinia. Here he bred Boar to be hunted. Hunting Wild Boar became very popular among the Romans in the Third Century BC.

Stretching back from before Christ, Boar hunting was always the preferred big game adventure throughout any continent where this animal could be found. European countries today still keep up the traditional style Wild Boar hunts developed over hundreds of years. From the dogs, to the man drives and standards, to the Branch in the mouth of the Boar after the kill as a token of respect, this animal has always been seen as an honorable pursuit.

When the age of exploration came we would soon see this mighty game animal spread all over the world. He would then become the preferred animal to be hunted by Alfa Male men from New Zealand and Australia, to Hawaii and the Philippines, and of course to the United States of America. Here it would find my family, the Kemmers, and eventually infect my father Norman. He would become obsessed with it, both due to it's pursuit with dogs, which he loved, and it's dangerous thrill which he grew to love even more.

My father would develop a relationship with the American Pit Bull Terrier which would eventually lead him in two directions. The first of these directions would be the hunting of Wild Boar. Through this he would grow to earn the same respect for this animal that Kings, Nobles, and Soldiers throughout history have. As a boy my father was raised hunting every type of animal that the Southeastern United States had to offer, but after being introduced to hog hunting with Pit Bulldogs, it would become his only hunting passion. This passion would eventually infect me for the whole of my life.

I wanted to take the time in this first chapter to reveal to you just how respected and honored the Wild Boar has been since the beginning of man's existence on earth. Now I want to explain to you it's spread world wide, but especially to the United States of America, and then share with you many of the adventures that this regal adversary provided for me and my father. I hope you find it to be as interesting as it actually was. A story of tough men, tough dogs, and of course tough hogs.

Chapter 2

Wild Boar Hunting and Its Rise in the United States

Hunting Wild Boar is an ageless classic all across Europe and most of the civilized world. To say it is a Sport of Kings would be an understatement. Wild Boar hunting can be found on cave walls throughout Europe, Russia, and Asia. It can be found on countless canvas' of paintings about ancient countries and their cultures. At one time in the world Wild Boar hunting was viewed as the most regal of hunts. Today all throughout Europe, Russia, and Asia it is still a sport for the wealthy and a time honored tradition.

Just like the wolf was domesticated into our modern day dogs, the wild boar was one of the very first animals to be domesticated. He was, and is today, one of the heartiest of all animals. He is omnivorous, which means he will eat plants of any kind, but also eat meat. He is a survivor far and above most animals, and this caused his quick spread around the world in the age of exploration. When the primary world of exploration started the four main players were England, France, Portugal, and Spain. Now on these long voyages the primary concern was having enough food to sustain ones journey. So eventually the plan was hatched to find a way to place food everywhere explorers might travel. Many of the islands in the ocean were simple volcanic islands in the middle of nowhere and had no animals on them to provide explorers with food along these stops. The search then began for an animal that could survive in any climate, from the cold of Iceland to the humid climate of a tropical Island. The ever resilient hog was the easy choice, and so began the spread. Hogs were brought on every ship setting sail. Some were eaten along the way but at every stop of a new discovery a small heard of hogs were released. Then upon returning to the same island years later, a food source for the sailors would be there. It was often said that when landing on what was believed to be a newly discovered land, the true tell tell as to whether or not you were the first to find it was to see if it had hogs on it. If so, someone had found it before you. This is why today hogs are world wide on islands like Hawaii, Guam, the Phillipines, Australia, and yes the United States.

No hog is native to the United States. The first hogs brought to the United States were put here by Hernado Desoto in 1539. He dropped them in St. Augustine Florida. Twenty or so years later he did the same thing in the modern day Brownsville Texas area. These are the wild hogs that are throughout the Southeastern United States today. The word "Feral" means domestic that went wild. These hogs that Desoto released were the domestic hogs of that day and time. This is what I personally have always referred to as Desoto Feral Boars. To me they are just like a European Wild Boar in every way except one. They have the coloration of a domestic. They were not the domestic Boars that we think of today on someones farm. We have spent almost another 500 years selectively breeding to get these big monster Ferals of today. These were closer in size to a European Boar when Desoto released them, but they had been bred domestically long enough to get a lot of the domestic colors. Also what makes them so close to a European Wild Boar today is that once they were released into the wild they immediately began reverting, through natural selection, right back to the original Wild Boar that they came from, and today they have spent almost 500 years doing that.

Now I have seen some ridiculous scientist that say that a hog reverts into a wild hog physically within his lifetime. He will say that a small pig taken from the wild and put in a pen at a few weeks old, will grow a shorter snout, than if he had remained in the wild. Also that if a domestic pig is released into the wild that his hair will grow longer and his snout will grow longer than if he had been pen raised. That my friends is straight lunacy. The length of your nose, color of your hair, your height, etc. are all determined the minute the sperm hits the egg in procreation. This return to the wild, if we want to call it that, does happen but over a long period of time. This group of hogs that Desoto released, for example, the ones with the longer snouts, thicker hair, better teeth, tended to survive better. In turn they lived and reproduced. Then the ones of their offspring with similar traits to help them survive did the same. So over many generations snouts got longer, hair thicker, and teeth better. Hence these boars of Desoto's were not only 500 years closer to their European Wild Boar decedents, than what we think of as domestic today, but they have spent the last 500 years reverting right back to what they came from. So today we see the same size, shape, and many other attributes of the European Wild Boar.

The purest of these original Desoto Feral hogs that can be found are the Ossibaw Island Hogs. They are protected today by many Wild Boar enthusiasts, including myself, with the help of the "Livestock Conservancy". The Conservancy does everything in it's power, with help from members like myself, to hold on to old lines of traditional breeds. Ossibaw Island is off the Coast of Georgia and was a spot where Desoto dropped off some of these first animals. Being an Island it was cut off from later growing civilizations on the US mainland. The Desoto hogs on the mainland would later cross with hogs put in the woods by famers, etc. and certain cross breeding began. The Ossibaw Island hogs however remained pure bred for hundreds of years. Myself, along with the Livestock Conservancy, also try and maintain what is today known as a Choctaw Hog, which are decedents of the originals that Desoto dropped near Brownsville, who eventually worked their way into the Choctaw Indian Nation in Oklahoma.

Some of the first Pure European Boars ever brought to the United States were brought here in 1912 by an English business man named Gordon Moore. He worked for the Whiting Manufacturing Company. He came up with the idea of starting a Hunting Preserve in the United States to bring his clients to. He brought in a small group of European Wild Boar from the Ural Mountains of Russia. He fenced 500 acres in the Snowbird Mountain Range on the North Carolina / Tennessee border. In between Murphy, North Carolina and Tellico Tennessee. The hunting area went on for years and then one day they decided to do a Horseback style English hunt for the Boar. The pressure drove the Boar through the fence and into what is now the Great Smokey Mountain National Park, where decedents of these Boar still thrive today.

Another interesting note on these original European Boar is that they were the first to be in the US, and since they came from Russia, folks in America now refer to them as "Russian Boar". To people in other parts of the world, they are known strictly as European or EurAsian Boar, but we call them Russians. So if you have always heard both terms, now you know the difference.

As colonization started in the US, most farmers ran their stock loose in the woods. Cattle, goats, and yes hogs were loose in the woods. The farmers would notch their ears to show ownership and others respected the system to a degree. The process was like what you saw if you watched the movie "Old Yeller", when they did the hog marking. My family, the Kemmer's, got into what is today Cumberland County Tennessee in 1806. They ran hogs in the woods in those days and this led to what would become a Hog Hunting Tradition in my family which has lasted until the present day.

These are wild free range hogs on Main Street in Crossville Tennessee in 1901. Crossville is the nearest town to Grassy Cove where my father's family arrived in 1806. This photo should prove to the Tennessee Wildlife Resources Agency that Wild Boar have been in Central Tennessee since this time frame and before.

Todays wild boar in the US is a combination of the original Desoto Ferals, Russians, and hogs that were ran loose in the different areas by farmers. My Grandfather, Charlie Andrew Kemmer, got his first taste of hog hunting by running hogs loose in the woods near his home in Grassy Cove Tennessee. Whether he was taking one of the family hogs in the woods to bring to the dinner table, or going out to do the spring marking of the ears, to show family ownership of the herd, he was a hog hunter. They ran Cattle, sheep, and hogs in the woods and at certain times of the year would take their dogs and round up whatever species of animal they were after that day. By giving the dogs a certain command, the dog would round up all the hogs, or all the cattle, depending on the command he was given.

This is my Grandfather, Charlie Andrew Kemmer, with some of his hog dogs as a young boy. This would have been around 1930.

Now as you will learn, a Wild Boar, is a worthy advisory for any man or dog. Tough, mean, vicious, and he has what constitutes knives sticking out of the sides of his mouth. This toughness would draw daring men like my Grandfather and his boys to make this their primary hunting passion. My Grandfather shared many stories from these old days of marking family stock and also from just hunting Boar for meat, but my favorite one was him and his good friend Kemmer Manning. (Yes Kemmer's first name was a result of his family knowing our family and thinking that our last name would make a good first name.) Kemmer was a big man and always wore an overcoat which he chose to only button the top button on. This caused the bottom of the coat to kinda flop in the breeze. One day him and my Grandfather bayed up a big mean Boar in a mountain side ivy thicket. Now the pack of cur dogs that they had were very rough and tough and had caught many wild boar in the past, but this boar had them backed off. He was big and bad and ready for combat. These cur bred dogs would not touch him. Not wanting him to get away, and not having brought a gun, due to the fact that this pack of dogs had always caught anything they were up against, Kemmer decided that he would just wade in and catch that boar. He felt that when he got close the dogs would get embolden and charge in as well. Well he was wrong. As he got close enough in the thicket for the boar to see him, the boar charged and my grandfather said that that ivy was about four foot tall in that thicket and that when Kemmer came out of there he was walking on the top of that ivy like Jesus walked on water. He also said he would never forget the bottom of that big overcoat flapping behind him. He said it looked like superman flying over that ivy thicket and that coat was the cape.

As World War two broke out my grandfather would lose many of his hog hunting buddies from his youth. Some died on D-Day, others on battlefields in France, some lost in the Pacific. My Grandfather would fight first as a driver of Landing Craft for the Navy in the Pacific. Then due to his wounds he was put on an Escort Carrier the USS Marcus Island, where he would fight out the remainder of the war in the Pacific taking part in major battles like the one at Layta Gulf. Never losing his love for hunting, he decided to stay in the military, joining the US Air Force when it began in 1947. One of his last stations was at Keesler Air Force Base in Biloxi Mississippi. He had two boys, my father Norman, and my uncle Jack. When they got to Mississippi my father was in the 9th grade. After his graduation from High School, my father did a four year hitch in the Air Force as well, most of it in Germany. Then he returned to the coast and married my mother and remained in Gulfport.

Being a tough alfa male my father soon became associated with a dog called the American Pit Bull Terrier. Now today that breed is widely known, but in 1968 few had any idea what this dog was. The sport of dog fighting, Bull Baiting, and Bear Baiting were what these dogs were bred up for. Dog fighting was as old a sport as any in mankind. Bear Baiting, the catching of a bear with dogs, at one time was the most popular recreational sport in all of the European Continent. It was said to have been introduced by the Romans. This American Pit Bull Terrier had been bred for such sports. Hundreds of years of breeding for what is referred to as gameness. Gameness is a willingness to continue combat, denying pain or regard for your own life. It is the willingness to keep going beyond reason. Simply put, by a man like myself.....it is beautiful.

Bear-baiting is thought to have been introduced into England by the Romans. During its heyday bear-baiting was the most popular diversion in the country.

Until it was outlawed in 1835, bear-baiting remained a popular as well as a legal form of recreation. But by the end of the 18th century, this pasttime — once the pleasure of Kings and Queens and highest nobles in the land — was almost exclusively patronized by the working classes.

Now my father had been weened on hog hunting stories and raised with a love of hunting them with dogs. He also remembered stories like the one of Kemmer Manning and my Grandfather (who I refer to as Pa), running across a Boar from time to time that even their tough seasoned cur dogs would not catch. To tough men like my father and my uncle Jack, with German and Irish blood coursing through their veins, those tough boars were the kind they wanted to catch the most. With this new found American Pit Bull Terrier, they felt they were on the right track.

Daddy began searching all over South Mississippi for guys to take him hog hunting with his new Bulldog named Hud, after an old Paul Newman movie. Now just like giving away a good fishing whole to a friend, no one wanted to take Daddy hog hunting. Not only did these old time hog hunters in the area not want any competition, but they did not want anyone knowing their prime hunting areas. As Daddy searched and found a place here and there, my uncle Jack, younger than Daddy, soon returned from his four year hitch in the Navy (most spent in Vietnam), to join him. Now a very cool thing happened for them about this time concerning a State Law in Mississippi. See Mississippi, like all Southern States had always allowed the running of stock in the woods, just like Pa had grown up doing. But each State then passed a "Stock Law". This law said that any farm stock, Cattle, Goats, Hogs, etc. not in a pen on your property was fair game and did not belong to anyone. Tennessee passed it's stock law in 1940, but Mississippi did not pass theirs until 1968. They gave everyone a year to get their stock up, but after that it was on the open market for hunting. Then Hurricane Camille hit and the State of Mississippi extended the deadline for an extra year. Now prior to this, to hog hunt in the woods you had to know places to hunt where the hogs were not claimed, or marked. After this, if a hog was in the woods he belonged to whoever caught him. Since everyone in South Mississippi who had farm animals had them running loose in the woods, hogs were everywhere. By running stock in the woods, they did not cost anything to feed. So a poor man could own hundreds of hogs, but if he penned them up, he could not afford to feed but a few. Catching them all for a farmer would have been impossible, but if it were possible, it wouldn't be affordable. So most folks left them in the woods. So in Daddy's beginning he could not hardly find a place to hunt, now he could hunt anywhere.

Mitch Kemmer at about age 3, with my crew of animals. The spotted bulldog pup just in front of me is the Hud dog.

When Daddy first started hunting after the stock law deadline, Interstate 10 was being built through South Mississippi. In the track of the Interstate was a town called Diamond Head. In Diamond head was one of the largest stock owners in all of the area. He had hundreds of cattle, sheep, and goats, but he had thousands of hogs. He was rich in stock, but poor in money, so when the stock law passed he had to let all his stock stay out, which unfortunately put it all up for grabs. I-10 at the time was just a dirt mounded, red clay road, not yet paved, but it went right through this guys area in Diamond Head. It was the easiest hog hunting Daddy and Jack would ever enjoy. Driving down an all but paved road, 200 feet wide and miles long, in the late evening and early morning, seeing hogs all in the road and median, and turning the dogs on them. Seeing a bigger one just down the road, and picking up and making a move on him. It was, as German submariners in early WW II called, "Happy Times". Life was good and easy and they got their start.

The Hud dog that Daddy bought as a pup, and was his first pure bred American Pit Bull Terrier, was amazing. It being their first, they just assumed that all of them were created equal, but later in life after having hundreds of Bulldogs, they would come to look back on Hud as one of the top three catch dogs that we would ever own. Many think that catch dogs are a dime a dozen and all they have to be is tough and willing. Those people are idiots, and know not what they say. There are all different degrees of all aspects of a catch dog. Some have better noses than others. Now a bulldog can not usually smell as good as a hound or even a cur dog. They were not bred for hundreds of years for trailing ability, they were bred for toughness and grit, but some can smell better than others. Speed is another asset of course, just like people, horses, etc., some are faster than others. Then there is athletic ability. Getting through the woods well, maneuvering, but mainly athletic ability in a catch dog means that he can get to, and catch, what he wants, and not just grabbing at what he has to. But mainly it is being able to actually catch and hold. I call it being able to 'snag'. Many dogs fumble and bobble a catch and lose their prey. When a dog can snag, that means if his hair touches that hogs hair, that hog is caught. Hud would be the best at all of these things. He would later have a pup called Judge, that was near his equal, and later in life a male called Ottis that was the same, but Hud would become the Coca Cola that we compared them all too. He was the bench mark. He was outstanding, he was beautiful, and as my Daddy would describe him .... he was magic. No hog could escape him. If he locked eyes on it, it was over. I saw hogs be 40 yards from the woods, us turn Hud loose 100 yards from the hog, and the hog break for the woods as soon as we released him and the hog not get to the wood line. Hud would cover 140 yards before the hog could cover 40. He was like a stick of dynamite and he spoiled us.

Our second real hog dog was a half Boxer and half Pit male we named Hombre, after another Paul Newman movie. We began hunting Hud and Hombre together, and murdering hogs. We then collected several more pure Bulldogs and bred Hud to some of them. We were on a roll with some rough tough catch dogs. Now every other hog

Norman Kemmer's Hud. This is the first pure American Pit Bull Terrier that Norman ever owned.

hunter on the Coast at the time used bay dogs. A bay dog is a hound, or cur, with a good nose to trail up and find the hogs. He then barks at, or bays, the hog then the catch dogs come in. Well Daddy was out catching them all in those days and we did not even have a bay dog to locate the hogs. We were doing the tracking and trailing until we found the hogs. All those old local clucks who would not allow Daddy to hunt with them, were now watching him come home with three and four times the harvest they had. The Diamond Head hunting was a turkey shoot, but Daddy and Jack started venturing out to all the local swamps and countrysides. They were hitting Louisiana and Alabama in these early days as well. They went anywhere they heard rumors of hogs. Friends and old High School buddies started joining them. Men like Drew Favre, LE Parker, and Wayne Parker. They were catching hundreds of hogs a year.

Now the main thing to know here is that none of this hunting was done with a gun. They were catching these hogs alive, tying their feet together, and carrying them out on their shoulders alive. My father never hunted hogs with a gun. He hunted with dogs and a four foot piece of string, and he was eat up with it. My Pa always hunted hogs, but he also hunted Deer, Rabbit, Squirrels, Turkey, etc, but all my Daddy and uncle Jack hunted was hogs. The other was too tame for them. As a child I was raised with a wide education of hunting everything under the tutelage of my Grandfather, but if I wanted

Norman Kemmer in the center holding Hombre, with Mitch Kemmer to the left and Marty Kemmer to the right. Hombre was mean, and in true Boxer cross fashion he was grouchy. Pure Pits either whip your butt, or they don't, but curs and cross breeds woof and snort and cause trouble on a hunt. Hombre was a trouble maker true to his pedigree.

to hunt with my Daddy and Uncle, I went hog hunting. It was thus all my father's life. He became so famous for it that local papers would do articles on him and his hog dogs as far back as 1972.

Now a hog by instinct is a pack, or herd, animal. When threatened it is in his nature to group up with other hogs to defend the heard. This instinct was never more evident than in these early days after the stock law had been passed. If you could catch a hog that squealed, every hog that could hear him would come to help him. Daddy and his crew would love to catch a small hog, tie him up, then get the dogs off and stand ready facing in all directions. Then bump the caught hog to make him sing out, then watch for oncoming hogs to snag. It was plenty sporty in those days because a big boar might run up your back while you were catching another one, or ten might come in on you at a time. It was a very exciting time to be a hog hunter. In later years this all stopped. Many said it was because the hogs learned not to come. The truth was that we were catching all the ones with the heavy packing instinct, and the ones without it were living and reproducing. After a while that habit stops due to natural selection. But it was fun while it lasted. On one of their hunts in Diamond Head while catching a young hog, they looked around and here came a big Possum Blue colored Boar right at them. Jack spun around just in time to attach a catch dog to him before being ran over. Daddy was never a keeper of trophies, but did cut the snout off that Blue Boar and put it in the freezer. Later in my life I would mount those teeth with another Boar cape, and it hangs in my Hunting Lodge today. That Boar was caught in 1972 and those teeth are still some of the very best I have ever seen in my life.

Later in life my father would get into other sporting aspects with the American Pit Bull Terrier and we would learn what the proper 'preforming weight' of a dog should be. That is the perfect weight at which he needs to be for combat. So in the future when you hear me refer to a dog as a 37 pound dog, you will understand my preciseness in this issue. What we would eventually learn through a lifetime of hog hunting was that we liked our catch dogs to be from 35 to 45 pounds. Anything under 35 pounds could not hold a big boar by himself. Not big enough, feet were not long enough to touch the ground when holding an ear, etc. They could be tough as a 20 penny nail, but the size was just not enough. As for the top end of our weight criteria, we marked that for several reasons. We found that anything from 35 to 45 pounds in a bulldog could catch any hog on the planet and hold him, so why go bigger than what you need. Now in most things in life, we were the king of overkill but not in this one. Anything over 45 pounds eats more dog feed, shits more, etc.. He is heavier for you to load in a box, load in boat, harder to lead because he is dragging you. He also makes a great deal more noise moving through the woods. See as hogs got to running more, and got spookier from being hunted, you want a nice quiet, athletic dog to be on the hog, before he even knows he is there. Big gaudy 80 pound dogs are way too fat, clumsy, and make to much noise to 'slip' up and surprise anything. Also he is a bigger target to the Boar. When a small dog has a hog by the ear, he has about a 5 inch wide chest right there beside those razor sharp tusks. With an 80 pounder, like some people like, you have a 10 to 12 inch target. A 40 pound dog to us is the perfect size to match all the criteria that we wanted, and brother I promise you there is not a Boar on the planet that I can not catch with a good 40 pound catch dog.

The little Hud male that my father started this type of hog hunting with was a 35 pound male. He was the reason that we set our bottom end of what we liked at 35, he could catch and hold successfully any boar there was. He caught his first hog in the woods at six months old. Then as we added to our attack crew with Hombre, and later pups off of Hud, he sure was a fine male to help get other catch dogs started with. Now Daddy had built up a pretty good little group of six to eight catch dogs at this time. One Saturday morning my Pa told Daddy that he had been seeing some hog sign in a spot near the house. Daddy took Hud alone to check it out. Daddy and Hud ended up catching and tying a big black boar around 290 pounds. After breaking Hud off Daddy realized that Hud had been hit with a straight on shot from a tush in the chest. A dog has a brisket bone in the front of his chest, and on each side are two 'sink holes', if a decent sized tush from a mature boar hits one of those sink holes, the dogs heart is just inside there. If he gets hit with a good shot in one of those sink holes, his heart will be punctured and he will be dead in about twenty seconds. Daddy lost Hud that day. Killed in action on the very day he turned 22 months old. Hud had been there from the beginning during the 'happy times' right after the stock law. He had racked up 264 hogs that he had caught from 6 months old when he caught his first, to 22 months old, and his death. Hogs were flowing like a river right after the stock law and had never been hunted, so they were easy pickings, but still 264 was an incredible number for any dog, especially when killed at 22 months. Again, I cannot overstate what an incredibly talented catch dog he really was. He was the catch dog that we compared all others to in later life. We would lead a life in the hog hunting profession that would see us with hundreds of catch dogs. Hud would rank in the top 3 that we ever owned ourselves, and we would see another in the hands of a friend that was his caliber. Real dog men often say that a man is lucky if he owns one good dog in his life, Hud was that dog for my father in his Hog Hunting life. My father never showed weakness, I would grow to believe that he did not have it, but he was crushed the day he lost the Mighty Hud.

Chapter 3
Norman Kemmer and Blackie

As my father's rise in popularity and knowledge in hog hunting expanded, he started hunting with other hog hunters. He was in search of a Bay Dog. Even though they were outdoing the competition, and having a ball doing it, he knew that hog populations would soon get thinner and thinner and a location dog with a good cold nose would mean the difference in success and coming up empty. Now Daddy never would hunt with the men around our area that refused to help him in the beginning. My father was very loyal to men who were good to him and very cold to those who were not. He soon hooked up with a hog hunter named Ed Gober.

Now ole Ed was a character. If he ever held a job it was unknown to my father. All he did was hunt hogs. He had a pack of dogs and a vehicle, which him and the dogs slept in when he was not hunting. He always kept 10 or 12 dogs and they would just swamp a hog, but he needed Daddy because among all his dogs he never had a good solid tough catch dog. He just had a pack of old cur dogs, much like the ones Pa hunted with as a young man. So when he ran on to a good tough Boar, he could not catch it. So him and Daddy made a good team for a while. Now Ed had a whole slew of dogs, but he had one that stood out above all the others. It was a little knotty, cross bred nothing of a dog to look at named Blackie. As him and Daddy started running together Daddy always noticed that it was always little Blackie that seemed to find all the hogs first.

Hunting with Ed went on for about a year and then one day my father hit a stroke of luck. Ed got to needing some money and wanted to sell some dogs. Daddy offered to buy Blackie. Ed agreed and wanted $150 for him. Now this was in the early 70s and $150 was a lot of money. My father was a brick mason and barely brought enough home each week to pay the light bill and keep us fed, so he did not have that much to spare. He then went to my Grandfather. Now being a lover of hunting and hunting dogs, Pa understood the value of a dog. When Daddy explained the situation and that he needed to borrow the money my Pa looked at my father and asked, "Is he a good one?". My fathers reply was, "He's the best". Pa then said, "Well, we better get him then". With that Blackie was ours. Ed soon moved away and Daddy never hunted with another man again to amount to anything. Many hunted with him, but Daddy had all he needed to become a real hog hunter.

Now there are many theories on the best way to hunt hogs. Some believe that if you run him long enough with a pack of dogs he will eventually stop and hold bay. That means stop running from the dogs and stand his ground to fight. Once a catch dog touches him he is caught. Some use "Open Mouth" bay dogs, meaning he barks when he first smells the hogs scent. My Grandfather was a big fox hunter. He ran packs of hounds that would run a fox all night long, 13 to 15 hours at a time. So my father and grandfather decided to see if this worked on hogs. See if the dog barks while he is trailing the hog then the hog hears him coming long before he sees him. Then the hog starts running from the dog before the dog ever actually gets close to the hog, then the race is on. Daddy decided to try this, 'bark on the trail' type hunting. Pa had some long legged dogs that could really put a chase on anything they were after, so off they went. My favorite story from these running days was a hunt out on Texas Flat road in Hancock County Mississippi. The dogs got after a boar, near where the car was parked. Texas Flat road was just that, flat as a pancake and you could see down it for a mile each way. We saw the boar cross the road on one side of the car with the hounds right on his butt. Then he proceeded to make a circle, which he continued for the next 9 hours. Soon he crossed the road on the other side of the car, dogs a little further behind him. Then on the other side a while later, dogs even further behind him. You get the idea. Then it got to the point that he got so far ahead of them by the end of the day that he had crossed the road on one side, then the other, before the dogs had crossed the first side. They joked that the boar was eventually going to catch the dogs in the circling fiasco. This Texas Flat road episode became typical of our experience with open mouth bay dogs. Now they did catch hogs with them, some held bay, but our theory on this style of hunting became that the boar only stops if he wants to. Many say, "Oh I have dogs that can stop him". We believe that no pack of dogs can stop him, unless he decides to stop on his own. So to anyone reading this book who thinks he has dogs that can actually force a hog to stop here is my challenge. Go hunt hogs in Ansley Mississippi. It is in the far South West corner of the State. Those hogs do not hold bay. So any hot shot that wants to prove me wrong, take your open mouth dogs to Ansley and you will catch them at dark, exhausted, and ready to go home. Good luck.

My grandfather was a dog hunter of every type of animal. He had some long legged Tennessee hounds that could run down most anything. These dogs ran foxes and coyotes until they gave out and the dogs caught them. It was legal to hunt Whitetail Deer with dogs in Mississippi, so my grandfather did. His hounds could push a Whitetail Deer to collapse. If his hounds had been after that deer for 2 hours, it could come by you on a stand and you could tell it was exhausted. Tongue hanging out, panting with every breath, you could tell he was tired. With a hog race, you never saw the hog tired. Dogs tired yes, but never the hog. He seemed to get faster and better the longer the race went on. Daddy always said it was due to his 'gate'. Now when a hog first takes off from a pack of close dogs he is like a Whitetail Deer or a rabbit, he is hopping over stuff, struggling, and hauling tail, but after he gets out in front of the dogs he calms down and sets a pace. A rabbit or a deer never do that, they maintain the panic stricken struggling run and maintain that until they give out. The hog sets a pace, and as my father put it, "has the easiest gate" of any animal. A hog does what we call a shuffle. Once he is ahead of the dogs, he calms down and in his run he barely even lifts his legs, he just falls into a little shuffle of a gate. Not leaping and bounding up and over bushes in a panic like every other animal hunted by dogs. He sets an easy, shuffle type pace and he can maintain it as long as needed. My father and grandfather used to try to put fresh dogs in the pack every few hours to keep up the heat, but nothing seemed to work, he only stopped if he chose to do so. He was not only a worthy adversary when it came to his toughness once he was caught, but as the calm hogs from the stock law days got scarfed up and we were hunting wilder and wilder hogs it became a challenge just to get a catch dog attached to one.

As an intelligent man, my father began to analyze the situation. He developed a plan to use a silent trailing dog who did not bark on the trail. This type of dog would not bark until he was looking at the hog. Since hogs are primarily nocturnal, meaning they feed at night, we would not hunt then. If you get after him with dogs while he is already up and around, then the race is on. The plan would be to hunt in the daylight when the hog was most likely in his bed sound asleep. The silent trailing dog would slip up on him in his bed, then and only then when he sees the hog, will he begin barking. We would also leave our catch dogs running loose in the woods with us. Train them to rush straight to the bay dog at the first sound of the first bark. The hog, fast asleep, would wake at the sound of the first bark, stand up, shake off, then start the debate, in his groggy sleepy state of mind, as to whether or not to run. Meanwhile from the first peep of the first bark, the cavalry is on it's way. The plan being to catch the hog in his bed before the third bark. Daddy called it, "playing for the fast break". To catch him before a race ever began. This is the hog hunting tactic that my father would use for the remainder of his life, and the one that I would argue, and we would prove, was the best to use for heavily hunted areas where hogs were 'dog wise'. By the time Daddy started hunting with Ed Gober he had developed this idea. When he saw the little Blackie male, he knew that this was just the type of silent trailing dog he needed for his plan of attack. After acquiring Blackie, him coupled with the pack of catch dogs he had been building, it was time to test the waters.

Training a catch dog to go to a bay dog is as simple as training a child that if he goes into the store there will be candy. As soon as the bulldog associates that bark with the fact that there is a hog at the end of it, he is hooked for life. We used to use our bulldogs as pups hog hunting, then do 'other' things with them for years, then take them back to hog hunting, and their first day back in the woods after years away, the first thing they did was stop every few seconds and listen for that bay dog. It was addicting to them, to say the least. It was beautiful, and simply poetry to watch, a good well trained dog do what he loves best. We always let our catch dogs run loose. Many hunters keep them on a leash and lead them up to a close distance to the bay dog before releasing. That allows the hog too much time to get his head together and decide to run. By leaving them loose they zero in on that bay dog. They realize that he is the one actually finding the hog. They watch him close, even follow him to some degree if they can. As long as they can see him they will move around relaxed, but as soon as he disappears from sight, they begin looking and listening to every small noise made. Then the first peep of a bark and they are off like rockets to him. Our catch dogs in the old days were so zeroed in on listening for Blackie to bark that we were hunting on a river one day and a boat on the river a half a mile away blew his horn, all three catch dogs that day with us had went to, and swam half the way across the river, before realizing that it was not a 'Blackie bark'. To say they were tuned into him was a bold understatement.

As far as the man getting ready with equipment for the hog woods it goes as follows. We had a dog chain for each dog. Never nylon type lead ropes, we put together chains made of 'Well Chain' that can be purchased at any Co Op or hardware store. Ropes of any kind can be chewed into in virtual seconds by a hard biting dog, then he is loose. Well Chain with brass snaps on each end attached with cold shuts. No quick links that screw shut, because if they screw shut, then they unscrew. As far as the length of these chains we made them to fit our chest. It goes over one shoulder and under the other arm and snaps. As for measuring the length, you lean forward with it, if it sags or hangs down from your chest, then shorten it. If it hangs down at all it will catch on limbs and briars as you are crawling into thickets. After removing a dog from a hog you snap one end to his collar and the other wraps around a tree small enough to get the chain around, but big enough that he can't jerk it over. After chaining him to a tree, as you start back to the action, swing wide of the dog on your trip. If you walk right back by him he may bite you out of excitement. Also tie him back at least 10 or more feet from the action spot so that you do not accidentally back into him while breaking another dog off.

As for ropes and tie string it is tricky. In the early 70s Daddy used something called 'parachute cord', but in the 80s the quality and strength of this cord went to crap. We eventually found a type of Kevlar String that was the size of this old parachute cord and was just as strong as the old stuff. Your tie string does not only have to be strong, but when you pull a knot, it needs to not be slick and slip back loose. I always cut my tie string a minimum of 4 foot long. That is too much for most hogs, but it is better to have extra length and not need it, than it is to need it and not have it. We threw a hog on his side, tied the bottom back leg first, bottom front leg next, then back top, then front top. If any leg will slip it will be the bottom front, because he is still the freest to struggle while that one is being tied, so it if any will be the one that does not get tied tight enough. People later used hand cuffs and we never liked that because it cut into the hogs legs. Later in the 90s we would use the quick tie nylon straps to some degree on small hogs, but we never trusted that loose dangling crap on a real Boar. The old tie method is still the most trusted. Sometimes we would tie a boar's mouth shut, if he had very long teeth. Now if he is carried properly and his head is left to dangle over your back, he can not bite or cut you. We primarily tied the mouth shut for travel in the

Boat. Boars with very long teeth can get to thrashing around in a boat and stick a hole in the bottom of the boat. When their mouth is tied shut it forces their bottom teeth and their whetters together and makes it a more blunt weapon. We also always kept a 'one legging rope' over our shoulders right with the dog chain. This is a thicker rope with a slip knot tied in it. The plan is if you get off and catch a big Boar by yourself then you hold the boar with one hand on the back foot. The hand this rope is set to slip over. Then with the other hand you slip this rope over your head and down the arm you have it slung over. Slip it over your hand, around the hogs ankle, tighten it and then back him to a good tree to tie him off to. Now when one legging a boar always tie the rope down low on the tree. If the boar circles the tree, he will tangle if he is tied too high. When tying a hog I always tell folks to "Tie it like you mean for it to stay tied".

During this time frame we were hunting a lot on the Pearl River, which in South Mississippi is the State line between Louisiana and Mississippi. One day we were hunting up around the town of Bogalusa Louisiana and we lost one of our catch dogs. His name was Little Hud, he was a pup off of 'the Hud'. When losing a dog Daddy would spend that night in the swamp where the hunt began. Most dogs that get off on adventures in the day light hours tend to break off from them at dark and work their way back to the place they were released. But after a night in the swamp and a several day search we just assumed that he had been killed by a hog or eaten by an alligator. About six months later, Daddy got a call from a friend of his that had been hunting with us many times. This guy had a friend at work that hog hunted a lot. He had been bragging about this great catch dog that he had, so Daddy's friend decided to go hunting with him. As the guy pulled up to his house they walked out back to load up his famous little catch dog. Upon seeing him Daddy's friend recognized him from hunting with Daddy. Now without going into great detail at this point let me simply say that my Daddy and my uncle Jack were two of the meanest sons - of - bitches to ever walk the face of the earth, and everyone that knew them, knew that. As Daddy's friend rounded the back of the house and saw Little Hud, he stopped in his tracks, threw his hands open and put them up in front of his chest, and said, "Don't get that dog close to me. I know the man that that dog belongs to, and I do not want to be within a mile of him, when he finds you with him." The man then began the story of how he found him with no collar on, of course, and did not know who he belonged to. Daddy's friend then said, "This hunt is over, and out of fear for my own life I will have to call Norman Kemmer and tell him that you have his dog. My advice is that when he comes to get him that you are not here." The man could tell from this guys attitude that he had stolen the wrong dog. When Daddy and Jack came to get Little Hud no one seemed to be home. They just went to the spot that they were told he was tied, and got him back. I was only a very small child at the time, but getting to know my father later in life and becoming very much like him and my uncle Jack, I always knew that that was not the end of that story. My father told it many times, as if the pick up of the dog was the end. They were the type men to tell that story that way to children and wives, but they were not the type to allow the theft of a dog to go unpunished. I never asked, but always suspected that after enough time had passed, that feller received another visit. As any true Southerner knows, someone is more likely to survive sleeping with a man's wife than stealing his dog in South Mississippi.

Little Hud would go on to be a part of a hunt that would hold a record over any other that we would have. Daddy went hunting one morning by himself. Being alone he limited the crew of dogs to a number he could manage. He brought Blackie as the bay dog, Little Hud as a seasoned catch dog, and he was woking in a new young 10 month old catch dog named Heck. The hunt was in a place north of our house called Red Gap Mississippi. They were walking in an open area when Blackie darted off in the edge of the woods and bayed. As the bulldogs rushed to the sound of the barking Daddy ran in. He heard a big 'thud' sound like hitting a bag of dog feed with a baseball bat. Blackie then went silent. See when the catch dogs catch then the bay dog will catch as well. But Blackie's silence only lasted a few seconds and then he started baying again. This was a bad sign, the noise of the thud coupled with Blackie's silence meant that a catch dog had arrived. The renewed baying after the silence meant the catch dog was dead and the boar was free again. Daddy then heard a dog whining back towards the clearing. It was Heck, he had gotten confused by a fence at the edge of the woods. Young pups sometimes have trouble crossing fences when they first begin hunting. Little Hud, being seasoned, had zipped right under it. Daddy then went to the fence and helped Heck over and turned him loose. A 10 month old new pup charging in on a boar that had obviously already killed a seasoned catch dog in a matter of seconds. Off Heck bolted with my father right behind him. As Heck reached the boar a sound that was seldom heard in the hog hunting woods by us began. It was a terrible screaming. The bloodline of bulldogs that we had were rawhide tough and would normally take their deaths in total silence, but not today. Later in life my father would tell me that only twice in his life did he ever hear one of our bulldogs screaming, and this day was the first. Heck was caught, he was 100% attached to the hog, and the awful screaming that he was doing was through his clenched teeth as he was holding on through a brutal brutal death. As Daddy rushed in to help him he ran straight in on the boar looking right at him. Heck was a hold of the ear and the boar charged straight at Daddy dragging Heck. Daddy then turned to run and fell, as he looked back expecting the boar to be on top of him, Heck had buried both front feet 3 inches in the ground struggling to stop this 400 pound monster boar. As the Boar stopped Daddy raced around behind him and grabbed a back leg. As he grabbed the leg, young Heck fell off his ear. He died within a split second of Daddy getting his hands on the Boar. Then this Boar proceeded to do something Daddy had never, nor would ever, see again. As Daddy held his back leg he began to pick Heck's dead body up in his mouth and shake him. Then sling him to the ground and do it again. He continued this until Daddy was able to get a rope around his back foot and get him 'one legged' to a tree.

After getting him tied to a tree Daddy was able to assess the situation. Little Hud, who had gotten to the Boar first, only had one hole in him. The boar had hit him one time. The Boar had caught him coming in and hit him right between the eyes. It was as if he had been shot with a rifle, he then went straight down. In a lifetime of hog hunting neither my father or myself would ever see a more perfect straight kill shot by a Boar than the one put on Little Hud. After getting Heck's body away from the Boar we found that he had 22 straight in holes in him. Most of which were in his chest. Both sink holes had been hit. His heart had been punctured several times. We would often remark that our blood line of dogs were good for holding a Boar until 5 seconds after they were stone dead. Heck would often be used as an example of this. A 10 month old pup, who had only been in on a few catches of small hogs, held this Boar and arguably saved my father's life on that charge, had taken a brutal butchering exactly like he was bred to do. Daddy would later return to the woods to work this Boar out of the woods alive. Now I refer to our property in Mississippi, which I still own, as 'sacred ground' due to the number of fine dogs that are buried there, but few dog funerals stand out in my mind more than that day we buried Heck and Little Hud. It was a somber ceremony and this Boar would hold the record of the only Boar to ever kill two of our dogs.

This is a good place to discuss different calibers of boars. As for meanness and toughness, I view boars like I view men. They are, contrary to an American myth, not all created equal. Some are just flat meaner and tougher than others. But also some are more athletic than others. Mean and tough is an easy trait to understand, they are violent, flip out into a rage, and fight as long as life allows. That covers the mean and tough aspect. But no matter how mean and tough they are, their ability to fight and put their tusks anywhere they want them to go depends on their athletic ability. Those tusks sticking out of the sides of their mouths are razor sharp on the edges for slashing, and when stuck straight into a dogs flesh, they are like being stabbed with a spear. But I have seen a many a mean and tough boar waller a dog, and sling him all over the place and never sink a tush in him. Getting just the right angle on him to make a good slash, or a good stick, is all determined by his athletic ability. A good talented boar can sink a tush clean to the gums in a dog every time he turns his head if he is an athlete. A boar can be talented just like a boxer, a race horse, or a good catch dog. Again, all are not created equal. This 'Boar from Red Gap', as he would come to be known, was like the Hud dog, he would become the bench mark that we compared the talent of all other Boars to. That straight in between the eyes shot he put on Little Hud as he came in on him was amazing, and something we never saw before, or after. Then to look at what he did to Heck. 90% of his holes were good straight in the chest shots, and not just an accidental slash from a scuffle. To do this kind of accurate damage, this Boar had Michael Jordan type ability and talent. He was, in short, a killing machine.

About a month later Daddy went back to Red Gap with a friend to hunt again. Blackie, bayed and as the dogs drilled into him they caught a big sow. As Daddy and his friend approached they saw a big Boar standing near the caught sow. Hearing her, he must have run up after the catch. Seeing the guys approach he charged them and ran them up a tree. He stayed under the tree for about five minutes, as Daddy's pack of catch dogs were proceeding to chew the top of that sows head off. Once a pack of dogs are attached to a hog they have tunnel vision and see nothing else. Stranded in the tree Daddy got a good look at the Boar below him. He said it was an identical twin to the Red Gap Boar that had killed Heck and Little Hud just a month before. Same size, shape, sandy color, and from all they could see so far, the same attitude. After about five minutes the Boar ambled off into the woods. Daddy quickly got down and broke a pup off of the original Hud dog off the sow. This pups name was Judge. Like Hud he was an ace. We would view Judge as one of the top 3 catch dogs we ever owned. That is why Daddy picked him to break off the sow first. He wanted to go after the Boar before he got away. Quickly locating the Boar Daddy released Judge. As Judge drilled him, the Boar just sulled up, just stood there, and gave up. They walked right up, grabbed his back legs, and that was it. What a disappointment. All that charging, keeping them up a tree raising hell, then when it come time for combat, he sulled up like a possum. This Boar was probably a litter mate brother to the one that killed two dogs, but they were not created equal. See when you are a tough guy, who makes a point of having tough catch dogs, it's tough competition that you go to the woods every weekend looking for. This second Red Gap Boar was a let down.

In these early years Daddy would own the best catch dog he would ever own, catch the single baddest hog he would ever catch, but also he would own the finest bay dog he would ever own in the little Blackie dog. It was a whirl wind of fine hunts and amazing stories on this little dog. He would do, know, and accomplish things that we would never see another dog, or group of dogs, do. Daddy always said he had radar for hogs. My only fault with him was that in some aspects he was too good. When you released him he went hog hunting. If there was a hog within a mile he would find it, if not he would range out further, if he came back after hours of hunting then you knew there was not a hog in a 10 mile radius. Now the issue with this, of course, was that in the early 1970s there was no such thing as a 'tracking colar", so if he went out of hearing and bayed you couldn't find him.....period. Also as a bay dog, he was game, he stayed bayed all day. If you did not find him he would stay bayed until about one hour after dark, then he would break off and come back to where you released him. As a very small boy I can remember spending hours in the woods after dark setting with my father around a camp fire waiting for Blackie. If you were hunting in a high populated area for hogs he was like a machine, you could stack them up, but if you were in an area with only a few hogs, one out of every three hunts would see you waiting on a bay dog until hours after dark.

Daddy and my uncle Jack were hunting one hot summer day in Belle Chase Louisiana. Now this place, at the time, was eat up with hogs. Blackie's routine was to bay the hog, catch him once the catch dogs caught, then if there were other hogs in the area, as soon as he laid eyes on Daddy coming in for the catch, Blackie would let go and go bay another hog. Many times we would be breaking dogs off, and tying a hog, and at the same time we would hear Blackie bayed on the next target. The magical thing about him was that if you got there and caught the hog, and Blackie did not turn loose and leave immediately, that meant there were no more hogs in that area. Well this day in Belle Chase the hogs were endless. They cut the dogs out and began catching. Blackie began the routine of cutting loose and going after the next one as soon as he saw the guys arrive. The action was hot and heavy going straight from one to the next. Also it was 'below sea level Belle Chase' in the middle of the summer, so Daddy, Jack, and the catch dogs were getting hot. By about the eighth hog they were roasting and about to pass out. When they left number 12 and headed for 13 Jack hollered at Daddy and said, "I am about to have a heat stroke". Daddy then hollered back at Jack, "Well then catch Blackie and not the hog". Then they both rushed into the pile grabbing for Blackie first, and the hog second. The only way to stop him in a place like that was to catch him. They caught 13 that morning as fast as they could run to them and tie them. Gameness in a bulldog means that he will not quit until he is dead. Blackie was the gamest bay dog I ever saw. The only reason he would stop an hour after dark is because he knew at that point that you, nor the cavalry were coming. See in a deep swamp, right at dusk dark the wind usually will lay and you can hear better than during the day. So many days, right at dark when the wind laid, we would hear him, where we could not hear him all day. So he knew that if we would ever hear him, it would be right at dark. If we had not arrived within an hour after total darkness, then he would come find us. Later in life when they came out with tracking collars in the 80s, Daddy would always say that he would have caught hundreds more hogs with Blackie if he had had them.

A story of Blackie's radar happened in Central Mississippi one day. Blackie bayed a group of hogs and as we ran in on the bunch, we caught one, saw six break off to the left, and a single hog break off to the right. As we arrive Blackie broke off to the left after the six hogs. We proceeded to catch them one right after the other. Then when the sixth one was caught, Blackie broke back to the right, went about two miles, and bayed the very same hog we saw break off to the right, and when we got to him Blackie stayed caught. So Daddy then looked at us, smiled, and said, "Well boys that must be all the hogs in this area". Blackie was as reliable as the sunrise and he had a sixth sense for hogs.

One of the very earliest hunts that I can remember was going with Daddy and mama to Chalmette Louisiana one day. Daddy always had trouble finding people to hunt with him. My uncle Jack drove an 18 wheeler for a living and was always gone. A good friend named Wayne Parker hunted loyaly with Daddy for about a year during these Blackie years, but no man wanted to hunt as much as Daddy did. So often mama would take to the woods with him. This day in Chalmette, they brought me along. I was 5 years old. On that day, by the time we could catch Blackie and stop him, we had caught 10 hogs. The coolest thing about that day was that all 10 were Boars, and not only that, they were trophy size Boars. All were between 165 and 350 pounds. Now that was just luck, but it was the luckiest we would ever be. Only caught 10 and all 10 were trophy boars. No sows, no shouts, and no pigs. What a fine day.

Daddy returned to Chalmette the following weekend with Blackie, and a Mississippi Highway patrolman named David Hammonds. That day they would catch the singe biggest wild Boar that we would ever catch in the woods. He was a little over 550 pounds and had 4 1/2 inches worth of teeth sticking out of his gums. Now we hunted this area of Chalmette for years and the mature big boars always averaged like everywhere else in the South that we hunted, around 300 to 350 pound. Those two 400 pound Red Gap Boars were monsters. 300 to 350 were very respectable boars, but the only way to describe this 550 pounder was just that he was a freak of nature. Nothing else we ever caught in those days was anywhere close to that size. Also they only used one bulldog to catch him with, but that one dog was Judge. They said when Judge hit his ear he was flipping Judge around up over his head like he was shewing at a fly buzzing around him. Judge was only 35 pounds. Now normally the routine is for one, or two of the guys, depending on the size of the boar, would grab a back leg. At that point then who ever is left will break off all the dogs and tie them to trees, then they flip the hog onto his side, and then tie all four feet together. On that day as they ran in on the hog, Daddy told David to grab the Boar while he broke Judge off, then they could tie the Boar. Well David was a big stout ole boy, way bigger than Daddy, and he had hunted

This is the 550 pound Boar caught by 35 pound Judge in Chalmette Louisiana. He was swatting Judge around like a fly, but he was caught. He had 4 1/2 inches worth of teeth sticking out of his gums. Norman Kemmer and David Hammonds were the hunters.

with Daddy before, but on regular hogs. When David saw the size of this Boar he asked Daddy not to break Judge off before they tied him. He said lets leave the bulldog on an throw this one together. That wasn't a bad suggestion on a boar that size. I was only 5 but I remember them bringing that Boar in alive and putting him in a pen at the house. He was a sight to see.

We got a call in this Blackie era that would see us go back to Belle Chase Louisiana and bay up the most hogs we ever bayed at a single time in our lives. Now usually a bay would be anywhere from 1 to 6 hogs at a time, sometimes on rare occasions we might bay 20 or so, but this trip to Belle Chase would see Blackie bay well over 100 hogs at one time. Now we hunted corn fields, soy bean fields, sugar cane fields, etc. that drew hogs in for food. But this monster collection of hogs in this single place in Belle Chase on this day was not due to any crop, it was to meat. A farmer had had a disease run through his cattle and his fields were covered with about 75 dead cows, and the hogs had come from miles around to eat those cows. Blackie bayed and Daddy and Jack stood and caught hogs until the catch dogs and them could catch no more due to exhaustion. Then they came back the next day and did it again. They continued this until the dead cows were all gone. Then the hogs in that particular area went back down to the normal numbers they had always been. It was the strangest thing, but the meat eating frenzy had pulled hogs in there from everywhere.

Norman Kemmer and Blackie in 1972. You are looking at the best of the best.

An entire book could be written on Blackie's exploits alone, but all good things eventually come to an end. Daddy was hunting one weekend up around Logtown Mississippi and lost Blackie. We had lost him many times for a day, even two or three, but on this day he never returned. Like with Little Hud, he may have been stolen by another hog hunter. As with many dogs that we lost, alligators were always a possible culpret. Or he could, of course, have been killed by a good, quick, accurate Boar. Whatever the reason, we searched for him for well over a month. Daddy never searched for a dog like he searched for Blackie. I remember riding with him many evenings to a place in Logtown were an old broken down train trussle crossed the Pearl River. I consider myself a real hog hunter. At one point in my life I considered myself to be a real Dog Man, but I have never considered myself to be a writer. But it is times like these, when I am summing up the life of a catch dog like Hud, a Boar like the Red Gap Boar, and a Bay Dog like Blackie, that I wish I was. Being a real hog hunter I know what these three animals were, but not being a writer, I can not convey just how fine, and rare they were. To say Blackie was far and away the best Bay Dog I ever saw in my life would not do it. If we are rating on a scale of one to ten, Blackie would be the ten, and the second best bay dog I ever saw would come into our lives in the 1980s. This little male in the 80s was named LE, and on that same scale he would rank as a 5. We would own a few others, and in the hands of other hog hunters I saw two more fair bay dogs, but none of the others I would ever see, apart from LE, would rank above a 3 on that scale. I would live to see three other catch dogs that were close to Hud's caliber, we would soon run on to another Boar that would be close to the Red Gap Boar, but no bay dog would ever hold a candle to Blackie. He was unbelievable. He was magic.

This photo was taken by a magazine crew in April 14, 1972. This article was done by "The Seabee Center Courier" which is a magazine put out by the Naval Construction Battalion Center in Gulfport Mississippi. The article was called "Gulf of Mexico Safari". It was about Charlie Kemmer, my grandfather, who was chief of police on this Seabee base after his retirement from the United States Air Force, and his son's Norman and Jack Kemmer. This photo shows Norman Kemmer and his crew of catch dogs at the time. Matilda is the brindle female walking behind Norman. We reference her in many stories. Dogs from left to right are Blackie, Grunt, Judge, Bo Jack, and Little Hud. Grunt and Bo Jack were two Pit / English crosses that we hunted for years. We found them to be slow and gaudy and we never used anything that big and cross bred again. Judge, the 35 pound brindle male in the center, was an ace and was always considered to be one of the top three catch dogs that we ever owned. Judge and Little Hud were both off of the original Hud dog. Little Hud was one of the two catch dogs killed by the 'Red Gap Boar'. I can not imagine a better photo to describe my father in 1972. When my mind flashes to these days, this is what I remember.

Chapter 4
BONNIE AND MO

Once we lost Blackie, it was back to hunting with just bulldogs. For years we would try, buy, and look at other bay dogs. The mistake with a lot of the bay dog culling we did in those few years after the loss of Blackie, was that we were looking for something of his Caliber. More than ten years later we would finally settle on the fact that his caliber did not exist on the planet, then we started hunting with bay dogs again. Of course we just settled on the best we could find and let it ride. But from the loss of Blackie in the early 70s until about 1983 we hunted basically with just bulldogs. This was a cool time in our hunting career because you really got to see what the American Pit Bull Terrier was. During the Blackie years they were all dependent on him. They just enjoyed a nice little stroll in the woods and waited for him to ring the dinner bell. But once he was gone, they really began to hunt. It all started in our search for Blackie in the four or five weeks after his loss. Daddy had two young catch dogs at the time named Bonnie and Mo. Every weekend after the loss, Daddy would go to Logtown. He decided to bring a couple of catch dogs with him so that if Blackie was there, they could just go on hunting. Once he would get there and Blackie would not be at the spot were we had released him, then Daddy would just go hunting. More for Blackie than hogs, but hunting none the less.

Well once Bonnie and Mo realized that they had no bay dog to rely on, they began really hunting. Now the bulldogs always hunted to some degree on close and easy stuff, but what Bonnie and Mo were doing was different. They really began to range out, and they both would prove to have some of the best noses that we would ever see on an American Pit Bull Terrier. On his first trip looking for Blackie, Bonnie and Mo caught two hogs, on the second trip they caught six, so the loss of Blackie was a lick, but truly we never missed a beat. Bonnie and Mo were on fire.

Bonnie and Mo were just part of our attack crew through these bulldog years. We did go through periods when we were trying bay dogs, but this time frame saw a lot of just straight bulldog hunting. This had it's advantages. There were no races, bulldogs do not bark on a hunt, by the time the hog realized he had company, he was caught. Also the hunter himself could dictate where you went to hunt. When you released Blackie he struck out and began ranging until he found the hogs. The hunter may want to begin in one spot and go West, for example, but if Blackie needed to cross a road, or a river, and go East, that's what he did. With a pack of bulldogs you went in the direction that you wanted, by not having as 'cold' a nose as Blackie, they had to be within a half a mile, or a mile to smell their prey. This worked out good because you have got to hear them when they catch, to know where they are. There is no baying bark, you either hear the first contact, you hear squealing if it is a sow or a young hog, or you are in trouble. The problem was that the big mature boars did not squeal, so little noise was made, and it was the big boars you had to hear or he would kill your dogs. See dogs don't kill a big fully mature boar, you either find them or he kills all your catch dogs. You can put 5 catch dogs on a boar like the Red Gap Boar and he will eventually kill them all if you do not get to the sight of the battle and assist your dogs. So in a way, this type of hunting was way more exciting and deadly than with a bay dog. Usually when a dog first makes contact with a big boar you will hear the contact, much like the 'baseball bat hitting the bag of dog food', sound that Daddy heard when Little Hud got to the Red Gap Boar. You may also hear a loud "Woof" sound. Many big boars will make that type of a sound just as the first dog makes contact. But many times you will not even get that. We have often heard simply the sound of brush being broken, or the sound of a struggle. One time I was hunting with Daddy and all three catch dogs disappeared. We knew they were caught, but could not hear them. At these points in a hunt we would be so still and quiet in our attempt to hear that no one in the hunting party was even allowed to breathe. On this day we started hearing a strange sound and when we focused in on what it was, it was the sound of breathing. Dogs with their mouths closed on a hog, teeth clenched tightly, and the breathing sound was them blowing and sucking air through those clenched teeth. Had it not been for us hearing that slight a sound, we would not have located them, which would have meant all of their deaths.

The mention earlier of this type of hunting allowing the hunter to dictate the direction of where the hunt went helped in another respect. If you watch television today and believed what you were spoon fed by the media, you would believe that hog populations are increasing every year and that soon the entire country will be over run with wild hogs and they will kill us all. Well this is as big a myth as is climate change. Of course they will show you study after study to prove the spread of hogs. This is an attempt by States and Insurance Companies to get Federal taxpayers dollars to combat something that is not going on. We will delve more into this in a later chapter, but suffice it to say that this hog population explosion is "Fake News". Immediately after the Stock Law was passed there were hogs everywhere. Hog hunting was like taking candy from a baby. In just a few short years however it became an actual hunt to find a wild hog, and eventually they could primarily only be found deep in the river swamps. The Diamond Head smorgishboard had dried up to some hard Marsh Hunting near there in a spot called Pine Hills. The hog numbers there were very thin, the hogs ran like rabbits at the sound of a leaf russleing, and it became a very difficult hunt to say the least. A few hogs can still be found there today, but had you seen the hundreds and hundreds that once frequented that area you would not believe the difference. Most by the time we were reduced to bulldog hunting in the deep south were found way in the river swamps of large rivers like the Pearl and the Pascagoula. Most of these rivers had been turned into Wildlife Management Areas. The flood zones on each side of the rivers made it impossible to build on, so the State used them in the best way they knew how. Well these Management Areas allowed hunting during hunting season, but not with dogs. Many of these areas had Game Warden Stations all around them. Hunting in there with a dog like Blackie might end you up bayed in the Stations front yard. Bulldog hunting went in the direction that the hunter decided, so we could swing way wide of such places.

This would be a good place to touch on the legal aspect of what we were doing. Now I come from a family that has a strong sense of honor, and right and wrong, but there is a big difference between right and wrong, and legal. Now we would never steal from a man, nor kill an innocent person, but if doing 35 in a 30 makes you an outlaw...... then outlaw we were....... and Daddy was the king of them all. My Grandfather had been Chief of Police at a Naval Base for 13 years after his retirement from the Air Force. He followed every hunting law to a tee. My father, on the other hand, only wanted to know what the laws were, so that he knew what to say when approached by a Game Warden. But hog hunting in Mississippi had many 'Grey Areas". First a hog was not considered a Game Animal, which meant that no game laws, nor seasons, applied to him. After the Stock Law deadline in 1970 any hog found in the woods, or out of his pen, was fair game to anyone in the State. Second, we did not hunt with guns. You could not accuse us of being in the woods with dogs to hunt Deer or Rabbits because we did not have a gun, bow, nor any equipment to kill anything with. We just had some pieces of string in our pockets. The only place we fell into a possible legal question in these State Management Areas was that they were no dog areas when it came to hunting. Well we could argue we were not hunting, at least any game animals, we were just in the woods for a walk. But since we never met a Game Warden we trusted to be sensible, we just felt it was a wise policy to avoid them all. This idea set in motion many wild stories for the remainder of my father's life concerning our hog hunting and law enforcement. I could never tell them all, but will attempt to sprinkle a few about.

Once I was on a hunt with my father and our cousin from Tennessee Johnny Mcculloch. Johnny was a big hog and bear hunter in Tennessee. Johnny's mama was a Kemmer, she was my grandfather's sister. Daddy had been hunting hogs for a few years in Mississippi when we heard that Johnny was hog hunting as well in Tennessee. So for the remainder of Johnny's life we would go hunt Tennessee with him on occasion, and he would do the same with us in Mississippi. On this day we were hunting on the Pearl River near Picayune Mississippi. Now some of the River Swamp in those days was still privately owned and okay to hunt with dogs, other parts were Management Areas. We had a habit of parking the boat on the private property part of the river and ending up in the Management part of the river to actually hunt. A common, and innocent mistake, I assure you. Well Daddy had gotten into a habit of scouting ahead as we neared the area that the boat was parked. No one could ever find us miles into a deep river swamp, but they might lay and wait to catch us at the boat. As we came up through the Management Area and neared it's boundary that day, Daddy had us catch up all the dogs, he then went out ahead and scouted. See we were hunting on a weekday due to being rained out of work. Well we had been hearing a very suspicious amount of boat traffic on the river that day, especially for a week day. As Daddy approached the boundary of the Management Area and the private land he realized that Game Wardens were scattered about every hundred yards or so along the boundary waiting for us.

It seems one had spotted our boat, then followed our tracks in the swamp mud to where we had crossed into the Management Area. He then raised the alarm and the steak out began. Well to put it lightly, my father was 'taylor made' for such events. After doing a little scouting, Navy Seal style, he discovered that they had about 15 Game Warden boat pulled up right on the river bank at the beginning of the boundary. Then the first Warden was out in the swamp right on the boundary about 100 yards from the boats. The Pearl River has the actual river, then the bank of the river at that boundary was up about 8 feet, so Daddy came and got us and we slipped right along the edge of the river bank, out of sight of the first Warden. We walked within six inches of their boats. We had trouble stopping the dogs from jumping in the boats. Then upon arriving at our boat, in a nice safe, dog friendly area, we built a camp fire and had lunch. When the Wardens saw the smoke and heard us laughing and talking, one of them shot down the river to check us out. By that point they knew they had missed us.

Another day Daddy was hunting in the same swamp with Wayne Parker. As they approached the boat Daddy left Wayne with the dogs. As he scouted slowly up to the boat he saw a strange boot track in the mud. He squatted silently and looked around. Just up the river bank about 100 yard he could see a strange small line of smoke rising slowly through the trees. A Game Warden had pulled his boat in under some bushes right on the river bank and was hiding, watching Daddy's boat. His mistake was that he decided to smoke a cigarette as he waited. After spotting the smoke, Daddy returned to Wayne. He told him to take the dogs about a mile down river and wait for him at a certain bend in the river that they both knew. Daddy would then go throw off the Warden and pick up Wayne when he could. As Daddy returned to the ambush sight he decided to have a little fun with our State Employed friend. Daddy knew exactly where he was from the smoke signals he had so foolishly sent up. Daddy slipped quietly right up to the edge of the Game Warden's boat. He had been so intently watching in the direction of Daddy's boat that he was not paying attention in any other direction. He had a hold of a big tree limb above his head and was leaning out of the boat, hanging practically in the river, trying to see around the bushes he was hid in. Daddy sat quietly for a few minutes then said in a loud voice, "Catching Anything". The sudden loud voice in the middle of that previously quiet swamp morning startled that Game Warden so bad he damn near fell into the river. Furious that he had been discovered, he then proceeded with a line of questioning. He asked what Daddy was doing. Daddy told him he was taking a walk. The Warden asked, "why are there dog tracks in your boat?" Daddy insisted that he did not know, maybe while he was out in the woods a strange dog came and jumped in his boat. The Warden demanded that Daddy give him a reason for being in the middle of the swamp all by himself. Daddy then remembered that him and Wayne had seen an old pile of bricks near there earlier that morning. Daddy then launched into a story about how he had been in there Deer hunting the previous year, during the legal season of course, and had seen some old bricks. His return on this day was to retrieve some of these bricks to build his wife a nice planter at home. Not being able to prove anything the Game Warden then sped off in his boat up the river. Now Daddy, being the king of caution in these types of situations thought that this foxy little cigarette smoking Game Warden might be the type to go hide further up river and wait for Daddy to pass, stop him again, to make sure all was as he had said. So Daddy retrieved a few hand fulls of these bricks, got in the boat and started for the boat launch. As he rounded about the second bend in the river, what do you know, out shot the trusty Game Warden from his hiding place in some new bushes, and stopped Daddy's boat. "Let me see those bricks", he demanded. So Daddy proceeded to show him the bricks. After another foiled attempt, he was forced to allow Daddy to go on his way. Daddy then proceeded to the boat launch, loaded his boat, and drove away. He then found a nice hiding place just up the road, and this time it was Daddy's turn to hide in the bushes. As the Game Warden loaded his boat and called it a day, Daddy returned to the launch, put his boat back in the water, and picked up Wayne, the dogs, and then the two hogs they had caught that morning and placed in strategic pick up spots on the river bank. Then off for home with another cool hunting story.

But it was not only Game Wardens that you had to face in those days. As you might expect, many land owners and farmers did not agree with the Stock Laws. Many still believed they owned the hogs loose in the woods. These rough old South Mississippi boys were way more serious than playing in the bushes with Game Wardens. When you are going West on I - 10 in South Mississippi from Gulfport, once you go through Diamond Head, you will cross the Jourdon River. If you look South of the Interstate, just as you are over the top of the River, you will see an Island. It is just a big Marsh Flat with only a few trees on it. For 10 years after the Stock Law passed there was a big sign on that Island that said, "If I catch you stealing hogs, you're a Dead Son of a Bitch". Now the hogs were perfectly legal to catch according to State Law, but who ever claimed those hogs on that Island did not think so. Boy we caught some fine ones out there. Several right under that fine sign. We never ran into the sign maker unfortunately, but in other places we were not so lucky. Or should I say, they were not so lucky. See people use to tell me and Daddy that the Game Wardens were after us, and Daddy would say, "Yeh, and if they ain't real careful they'll find us".

Some of the many Wild Boar we kept on our farm after catching them. In the back you can see a big Boar facing the Camera. This Boar was caught in Diamond Head Mississippi and was always ranked as one of the top five baddest hogs Norman Kemmer ever caught. He shredded 4 bulldogs in combat, but within a week of being at our house he would eat out of our hand through the fence. Some Wild Boar would calm down and some never would. If you walked up to this Boar in a pen and had a dog beside you, he would lose his mind and try to tear through the fence to get to you. If you came alone he would be calm.

Daddy and Wayne were hunting one day up in George County Mississippi. They had started the hunt on a friend of Wayne's from works place. But as the dogs chased, and trailed hogs, they headed through the woods. The dogs had disappeared and they began a search when suddenly they found themselves surrounded by 12 guys, all with shotguns. They proceeded to tell Daddy and Wayne that all the hogs in those woods belonged to them. Having guns got them to talking bolder and bolder, and louder and louder. See Daddy never carried a gun in the woods on a hunt, just tie string and dogs.

Daddy, realizing that he may not be on the land that he had permission to be on anymore, conceded that he may actually be on their land and as soon as he could find all his dogs he would go back the way he came. Then one of those gun toting country boys made a mistake. He said, "Well if I see one of your dogs, he is dead". Now knowing my father's quick and deadly temper, Wayne back out of the way from in between Daddy and the big talker with the gun. Daddy then flew into the man's face, and from there noses being two inches apart at this point, Daddy hollered, "What is your name?". The guy realizing that he had pushed the wrong button on the wrong man gun or not, lowered his head and said in a slow country voice, "Jake". Daddy yelled, "Jake what?" The man said, "Jake Green". Daddy then said, "Well Jake Green you better hope that all of my dogs come in to me this evening, because it they do not I am going to hunt each one of you down and kill you, and you are going to be the first". Daddy and Wayne then walked off in search of their dogs. Luckily for Jake Green and his crew of tough guys, they did find all their dogs by days end. Ole Jake better thank the lord that no Gators caught any dogs that day. After this George County incident Daddy began carrying a little 38 caliber snubbed nose pistol with him for the next 5 or so years. Not for hogs of course, but for men.

I was hunting with Daddy and another guy on the Pearl one day. We launched the boat from Bogalusa, on the Louisiana side. That day we caught a big black sow that had absolutely no ears. We lost a dog that day and after returning to the boat and he was not there, Daddy ran me and the other guy up to the boat launch to wait, as he ran the river banks looking for the lost dog. He dropped us off with the other dogs and the hog to wait at our van. As we waited an old man came to the boat launch. Seeing the sow near our van he asked where we caught it. Now I was only about 8 years old at the time, but being raised by an outlaw father and uncle, I knew the rules, mums the word. The older guy hunting with us that day also refused to give up the goods. He knew Daddy well enough to know not to make a verbal mistake as well, if only out of fear of my father. The man proceeded to tell us that he was going to cut her loose. Being only a very small child, but wanting to help, I said, "Mr. I wouldn't do that until my Daddy gets back". The old man then started to his pick up truck for a knife, as he opened the door I saw a pump shotgun laying across his seat. As he pulled the knife from the truck I looked and saw Daddy pulling up in the boat. I ran over and said, "Daddy there is a man up there wanting to take our hog". Daddy looked at me and in his Alfa Male Southern Voice said, "Well we'll see about that". I had known him long enough to know what that meant. As Daddy walked up the man asked where Daddy caught that hog. Daddy said, "It doesn't matter where I caught her, she is mine". The man then asked, "Don't you see those ears?" Daddy said, "No, as a matter of fact I don't see any ears". The man replied, "That's my mark, I cut the ears all the way off, that is my hog". Daddy then explained that it was not his hog, it was our hog and he had best step away from her. The man started to his truck. As he walked I told Daddy that he had a shotgun laying across the seat of his pick up. Daddy immediately headed for our van, reaching in from the passenger side he grabbed the 38 pistol that he had been carrying with us from the George County affair a year prior. As he looked back to see where the old man was, he realized that the man had not walked to his driver's side of the truck, as he would have done if he were leaving, he walked to the passenger side. As he reached over into the seat, arms outstretched in such a way as to tell anyone that he was grabbing that long shot gun, he looked back to see where Daddy was. At this point Daddy had the pistol, faced the man flat footed and straight on, had his arms at his side and in his right hand was the pistol. The old man saw it. Now in my lifetime I have known only a few serious men, you know the kind they make movies about. Well my father and my uncle Jack were two of the baddest on the planet. I knew that if that old man had come out of that truck with that shotgun that Daddy would have killed him. Luckily for the old man, he seemed to get the same impression. Half way up with the gun, he stopped, laid it back in the seat, to the driver's side he went, and away he drove. Daddy had found our dog, we loaded our sow, and we too headed home. One interesting side note to this story. When Daddy had dropped us off at the van earlier to go and look for the lost dog, he had put the pistol and most of his gear in the van to lighten his load. About half way home that day Daddy remembered that,at that point, he had unloaded the pistol. He had been in a 'face off' with an unloaded gun.

This Bonnie and Mo time of bulldog hunting would see us not only have fun with Game Wardens and people, but catch some damn fine hogs. My father-in-law David Mitchell was also my cousin. Yes I am a Southerner, and I married my cousin. I always remarked that I could never find a good enough bloodline to make an outcross to, so I went back to the family. But Dave's Daddy had died when he was 15 years old. He had always hunted with my Grandfather at every opportunity and they were very close. Upon the death of his father, my grandparents took Dave in. He moved from Tennessee and live with us until he graduated High School and went into the Air Force. He was ten years younger than my Dad, and I was 10 years younger than him, and now my wife is 10 years younger than me. But as Dave arrived in Mississippi my father and my uncle Jack were hog hunting hard. Dave fell right in. Him and my father were hunting one day on NASA land, in what is now the Stennis Space Center in Hancock County Mississippi. They had 5 catch dogs with them on this day and got on, what we would always refer to as the second baddest hog we ever caught. It was the dead heat of summer and this Boar had almost no hair due to summer time shedding. He had monster thick shields on his shoulders and all the way down his rib cage. We would always call him the Rhinoceros Boar. Now Daddy only had two dogs on the Red Gap Boar, and he had at them one at a time. This Boar had 5 dogs on him at once, and when they came running in on him they said it looked like something from a horror movie. The Battle had beaten down the brush in about a 15 foot circle, and they said that blood had the surrounding trees painted red up about 8 foot high. Once the Boar was tied, a closer inspection found chunks of meat hanging from tree limbs in numerous places. None of the dogs died from this catch but all 5 had been cut all to pieces, some with 15 to twenty holes in them a piece. Bulldogs can take an enormous amount of damage and live. Usually only a cut artery in the throat, or a straight on sink hole chest shot into the heart will kill them. Every now and then a rib will snap from a hard blow, and puncture a lung, but they can be cut to ribbons and live to hunt another day. This Rhinoceros Boar had not actually killed anything, but his ferocity, accuracy, and ability with 5 seasoned catch dogs on him at one time always made him stand out in the rankings of bad hogs.

We also lost a fine bitch in this time frame named Matilda. She had been a bad mouth catcher on hogs since she was young. Mouth catching is okay, but it usually causes the catch dog to eventually get all her teeth broken out. Matilda had lost all of her teeth at a young age. We always said she was slick as a goat. Now Daddy had gotten into other sporting events with his bulldogs shortly after becoming a hog hunter. He used Matilda in such events. See you can start a dog off young, teach them not to fight, teach them to hunt, then do other things with them, and bring them back to hunt and they will fall right back into the hunting routine. If you try other things first, they will most likely never be able to be broken from causing trouble. So hunt them first, but not the other way around. Daddy started Matilda hunting, so she was fine. He even competed with her one Saturday night, then took her hog hunting with other dogs the next morning. She was a fine gyp. On the day of her death Daddy and Jack were hunting on the Pearl. The other dogs got into a pack of hogs. Matilda was a ways away. Now usually all the dogs tend to get on one hog, due to the packing instinct of a dogs nature. But as Daddy ran into the battle scene, Matilda came running up from the other side to the group of hogs and ran face on with a big black boar. The Boar saw her coming, got set, and hit her hard coming in. With no teeth she slipped right off the ear and went flying backwards in the air. While in the air her feet were moving as if she were running. Upon hitting the ground, her feet already in motion, she sprang back forward like a rocket. The Boar had had the perfect amount of time to get set for her again. He hit her again and the motion through the air and than back again repeated itself. Then again. Daddy said that the rhythm that they had was uncanny, but he knew that every time she was getting hit, she was getting cut. A Boar that could set up a rhythm like this was a sure to the core athlete, and he knew what that meant. To help throw off the Boars rhythm and help with the catch Daddy ran up on the opposite side of the boar. As he took a glance at Daddy, Matilda nailed him and locked on. He was caught at this point but had cut her throat numerous times. She died within seconds. When they returned that night, my father lifted me into the back of that ole van. Hog tied in the floor, Matilda dead beside him, and he proceeded to give me a speech about bulldogs and how they should take their deaths. It was a speech that would impact my life more than any other single event. I would go on to box, play football, bare knuckle fight a ridiculous amount, and spend a life with bulldogs. This speech would be applied to my own life and I would use it in a lifetime of culling to find the kinds of dogs I wanted. Some say I took that speech too much to heart, some say it drove me crazy, some say it made me see everything as a battle field. I say it was a damn good speech given to a young kid with pedigree to understand it, and yes I saw everything from that day forward as a battle field, and I believed with all my heart that God Hates a Coward. Thank you Matilda.

When our cousin Johnny Mcculloch first came to Mississippi to hunt with us, he was hunting strictly with Plot Hounds. He had a whole pack of 15 or so Plots. His style was much like that of my grandfather's and of Ed Gober's, just to swamp him with cur dogs. That will catch most hogs if you use an entire pack of dogs, but from time to time you have to watch the occasional bad ass walk off, as in the case with Kemmer Manning. My father quickly decided to give Johnny a lesson in economics. Daddy asked him first to get his toughest plot hound and bring him to our barn. In a 20ft x 20ft barn stall we had about a 90 pound Boar. Not fully mature, not real good teeth, but a mean ass little dude. Daddy told Johnny to throw his plot in there and catch that boar. As Johnny threw that plot in that stall the damnedest hollering, screaming, and balling proceeded to resinate from that barn door opening as that little boar chased that 120 pound worthless Plot Hound all over that stall. That boar chewed that Plot up one side and down the other. I do not think there was an inch from the tip of that Plot's nose to the tip of his tail that that little boar did not bite a chunk out of. There was Brindle hair all over the floor of that stall when we were finally able to snag that cur out of there as he ran by the door. He would not lock on enough to get in there and catch the hog, so they just had to keep grabbing for him every time he passed the stall door until they finally got him. Johnny then said, "well let me throw 4 more Plots in there and we will get him". Daddy then went and got a 30 pound bulldog female pup that we had and as he walked to the stall door he said, "Now I'm going to show you how to catch a hog". As they cracked the door open the hog was standing right there facing them, and 'BAM' he was caught. That twenty minute escapade we had previously watched had produced nothing but laughter from me, Pa, Jack, and Daddy, and a split second with a real dog and it was over. Daddy said, "Now that's your lesson in economics. One 30 pound dog that eats 2 cups of feed a day can catch in a split second, what it takes you 15 100+ pound Plot Hounds to catch, and each of them eat 6 cups of feed a day each". Now most ole stubborn Southern country boy hog hunters would not admit that they were wrong, even when you can prove it to them, if it meant there deaths. But Johnny was not so dumb. He left our house that day with bulldogs from our yard and hunted with them until he died. His son Greg and his grandsons live in Maryville Tennessee today and still hunt with bulldogs. Those boys are true blue hunters.

Another good story from these days was a pup called Yeller. Daddy took Yeller to the swamp the first time when he was about six months old. The older dogs were out making a sweep of the area, and Yeller being new in the woods was staying under Daddy's feet. They then walked up on a monster boar sleeping in a woller. As the boar jumped up Yeller nailed him. He had never even seen a hog in his life. It was his first time to be out of his dog pen, and first time to be in the woods, and he nailed him. Good ones are born good. Yeller would turn out to be a super star in every endeavor we would try him in. About two month, and several hog hunts later, we were in the woods with Yeller and he had started venturing out. Well we lost him. We searched all that weekend, but usually if you haven't found them within two days that is it. Well three weeks later to the day after losing him, we were coming down the river one morning on another hunt, we rounded a bend in the river and there laid Yeller on a sand bar watching the boats go by. As we approached him he ran off, so Daddy sat down on the sand bar and waited. Yeller eased up behind him and as Daddy put his hand behind his back, Yeller smelled it, Daddy spoke, and he went hunting with the crew again that day. As Yeller matured Daddy would use him for other things, he would prove to be extraordinary in that field of sports as well.

One of my youngest son Norman's favorite stories that I tell from this time frame was the day we hunted the flooded swamp. I was 8 or so years old at the time and it had rained all week that week in South Mississippi. The swamps were record flooded come Saturday. Now on these flood hunts the goal was simple, hit the swamp and walk, wade, or swim until you hit the high ground. When you find high ground every animal in the swamp will be on it. Then it's hog heaven for a hunter with a pack of good catch dogs. Well we brought six bulldogs on that day. Now the down side to a flooded swamp is that the alligators can go anywhere in the woods undetected. We walked all day that day and never touched dry ground. No high spots because the water was just too high. The worst part was that we lost all six dogs that day to gators. The last dog, a buckskin male named Shine, was with us until we got within site of the boat. When walking through flooded swamps, if you come up on a section of water that is moving, then it's a stream, or what we call in the South a slue. As we approached the slue Daddy and the other adults dipped in and swam across. I, being a little kid, was in the back. Shine was with me. As I leaned in to swim the slue, Shine went in right beside me. When we reached the other side he was gone. 50 yards from the boat and 4 ft to my right as I swam, and down he went. We always lost more dogs to Gators in the deep South, than to hogs. It will make a hog hunter hate an Alligator. Six dogs gone in one day, it was a record.

One day Daddy and Jack were about four miles deep in the swamp and caught a big, tall, rangey, black boar. This Boar killed Mo. They were too deep in the swamp and caught him so late in the day that they decided to turn him loose because they could not carry him out that far alive, and carry Mo's dead body as well. They released the Boar. Hunting in the same area about six months later, they caught the very same Boar, and he killed Bonnie. They were deep in the swamp again, but this time killed the Boar and carried him out in pieces with Bonnie as well. He was a very recognizable boar because they said he had a large knot on his skull right between his eyes. They both said his teeth were so big they wanted to carry his skull out as well. Neither my uncle nor my Dad were men who kept a lot of trophies, but they wanted this Boars skull. After carrying it for over a mile, with three or more miles to go and darkness approaching, they made the decision to leave it. Getting Bonnie's body out so it could be buried on the sacred ground of our home with countless others including her partner Mo, was much more important. Honor above all things.

Now we got to a point in the late 1970s were hogs numbers were getting mighty slim. We re-released a lot back into the woods due to dwindling numbers, but contrary to that 'Fake News' that fills hunting channels today, when you hunt as heavy as we were in those days, you can thin some hogs out. We always ranged out to hunt Louisiana, Texas some, Alabama, and Northern Florida, but we were rapidly thinning the population. We went from catching hundreds in a year in 1970, to being lucky to catch one a weekend in the late 70s and having to hunt all day to do that. Daddy had also gotten into other dog related sports and due to the purchase of a world class dog to base a yard on, he was poised in the very late 70s to take over the world, and for the next six or so years.....he did just that. His return to the hog woods was due primarily to me. As a small child I was useless to him in the woods and only a burden when I tagged along. When I would be in the house during week days, if I heard him talking on the phone to someone about hunting that upcoming weekend, I would go set by him at the table while he talked. By doing that I knew that he would know that I had heard him, after hanging up I would do my best to make eye contact with him. If I did, to be polite, he would ask, "Do you want to go hunting with us this weekend". The answer was always, "Yes". As he took his dogs in another direction for years, I just waited for the day that I was big enough to hog hunt on my own. Raised hunting with him when I was allowed to, hearing the stories upon return when I was not, I was slap eat up with it. Meanwhile I hunted everything else South Mississippi had to offer with my Pa, but it was hog hunting that filled my dreams as I slept. One day I would drag my father back into it.

Before leaving this early 70s time frame of hog hunting with the American Pit Bull Terrier, let me mention one other bit of fun that my father and my uncle Jack took part in with these tough dogs. Even before becoming full fledged hog hunters they began catching wild Cattle for people. The passing of the Stock Law was for any farm stock. Farmers had always ran Cattle, Sheep and Goats, as well as hogs in the woods. The passing of the Stock Law had seen many cattle left wild in the woods. Even in my High School years in the early to mid 80s there were wild cattle still running in the woods in the Little Biloxi River Wildlife Management Area. In these early days of owning these tough Pit Bulldogs and looking for any challenge, my father and uncle began approaching farmers about catching their wild cattle for them. Now had we been in Texas they would have just sent a few cowboys in on horseback to rope and round up these wild dudes, but in the swamps, marshes, and thickets of South Mississippi and South Louisiana this was not an option. Therefore they would pay Daddy and Jack to go into the swamps, catch the cattle with dogs, tie a rope around the neck and back leg of the animal, tie him off to trees, then later the farmer would work his way in with horses and work them out. Daddy and Jack got so famous for doing this that they were placed on the call list for the Mississippi Highway Department to be called if a stock trailer turned over on a road and they needed the animals caught in short order. But there noted popularity for this talent was never so evident as when Angola, the Louisiana State Penitentiary contacted them to come to the Prison and catch over 300 head of Santa Gertrudis Cattle that was running wild in the swamps around the prison. The prison wanted them caught to feed to the prisoners.

Catching cattle was much more dangerous than catching hogs. We averaged losing two to four dogs a year killed by hogs, six to eight a year to alligators while hog hunting. but on average when catching wild cattle we lost one dog on each catch. So when Angola called Daddy told them not only could he not afford to take off work to do it, but he did not own enough dogs for that task. Cattle, especially the Bulls, were just dang big. They would jerk dogs teeth out, fall on them, stomp them, etc.. It was not that the bulldogs were not tough enough, that is a joke, but six 40 pound dogs can't stop, or even slow down a big bull. The bull ran until he decided to stop and fight, then Daddy or Jack would run up and put a rope around his neck. Never a noose type rope, because there were usually a couple of bulldogs attached to his face, but a rope with a big snap on it. They would have a knot in the rope to snap behind so that the rope would not cinch up and choke him. They would then tie him to a tree. Then another rope around a back foot, tie it to another tree, then start breaking dogs off. An entire book could be written on these wild cattle catching exploits alone, but I will touch on a few.

When catching animals dogs tend to have a place that they catch every species. They catch hogs on the ear, goats and sheep on the neck, and cattle and horses on the nose. Mother Nature gives them these 'catch instincts' that, as best I can tell are the perfect leverage points for holding. We have discussed talented catch dogs, as opposed to non talented catch dogs. They are not all created equal. It is the talented dogs that can get to these instinct catch spots because they have the ability to get anywhere they want to be. A non talented catch dog simply bumbles in and catches whatever he can. When the famous Hud dog would go after an 1800 pound Brama Bull in an open field, as it ran from him he would shoot right up under it, catch it on the nose, and as it's head was jerked down by this little 35 pound Pit, it would cause him to cut the prettiest full flip and roll you have ever seen. Yes an 1800 pound bull flipped completely over by a 35 pound dog. Now of course then the Bull would get back on his feet and run off with this little dog attached to him, but the flip was beautiful. Then as 'non talented' Hombre arrived he would catch the bull right in his nut sack, or in a back leg. The differences in their ability was day and night. The talented catch dogs were few and far between, and worth their weight in gold.

This talent could also be found in a Bull, just like it was in hogs or dogs. I have seen a good talented Bull go down through the woods with six or eight bulldogs attached to him and as he passed trees at top speed he would slide his face or his side up against that tree to try and scrape off an attached dog. The talented ones like Hud, or later Judge, never came off. The Hombre's came off and then caught again. Another strange thing about Wild Bulls was the question of breed of cattle. Most cattle are like most hogs, some are tough and some are not. Similar to the Red Gap Boar, then his brother a few weeks later. But there was one breed of cattle that were 100% insane, and that was Brama's. My father would spend a lifetime breeding dogs for toughness and gameness. It would be a constant struggle to keep up breeding standards to keep an insane, intense, kill crazy attitude that would take his death in combat walking forward into his enemies. Brama's were 100% this way all the time, bulls, cows, calves etc. They were impressive. We often wished we knew their secret to achieving any line of animal that was that consistent with their insanity. It was impressive, and deadly.

Once when I was very small we got a call on a Bull three hours north of our house. Daddy grabbed one young brindle female that we had and we took off. This female had never caught a hog or a cow, but showed a good attitude. As we saw the Bull he broke and ran. As this little gyp was released she ran right up under this big Bull going for the nose and he stepped right down into the center of her back and broke it. Her backend was lifeless, but she continued down through the field pulling herself with her front legs, and dragging her entire back end. It was a beautiful testament to what a real bulldog is. We caught her, then had to drive all the way home, get another dog, come back and catch this Bull. But that poor little brindle females mind was perfect, she often crossed my mind when I heard people make excuses for their dogs lack of grit.

Once we got a call on a stock trailer that had turned over on Highway 53 near Poplarville Mississippi. He had one 2000 pound Bull and 4 more in the 1800 to 1875 pound range. We knew that because he had just bought them at the local auction. It took all day, but we caught them all, while only getting two dogs killed. One of the Bulls was an 1850 pound Brangus Bull. We cut six dogs on him right off the Highway. As one bindle female named Matilda (Spoken of earlier) came in on him he hit her and flipped her so high up over his head that she hit the telephone line attached to the power poles 30 feet above his head. As she came down through the air, her feet in motion as if she were running towards him in the air, she landed in the center of his back. Being half Brama he had a big hump on his back. As she landed, she caught the hump, then the bull took off with all six dogs attached to him busting through fences. It took 45 minutes to finally run him down and get ropes on him. Matilda, being young and still having her teeth at this time, was still attached to that hump on his back and she had eaten a hole the size of a watermelon out of this hump.

Daddy and Jack did as much cattle hunting in the early days after the stock law, as they did hog hunting. As stock got caught up more and more over the years, they reserved themselves to just hog hunting when in the woods, but this was a very exciting time to be alive.

Over the years we would catch many things with the American Pit Bull Terrier but this cattle time reminded us of the old Bull Baiting of the days of kings. Men at these Bull Baiting events would breed a male dog to several females, then as the dogs would catch the bulls in these baiting events, they would break them off, cut off a leg then send them back in. This would continue until the trusty dog's death, or until all four legs were gone. This would show the dogs value as a breeder and bring a higher price for his pups. This was also done in Bear Baiting, which was introduced into European Culture by the Romans, and at one time in World History was considered the single number one recreational sport among the wealthy. It was events like this in our history that led to the creation, through hundreds of years of testing and culling, of the American Pit Bull Terrier that we began to know in the United States up into the 50s and 60s. A lack of proper testing and culling would see the gameness in this breed decline, but we were lucky enough in the late 60s to acquire some of these very fading traits. My father and myself would struggle to maintain this kind of gameness for many years. To rarely see it, and own it, was the rarest and truest of treasures for men like us.

In formal baits, the bull wore a heavy collar and was tethered by a long, sturdy rope. The dogs were expected to attack from the front and attach themselves to the tender flesh of the bull's nose.

Bull baiting was a sport of kings.

From a set of paintings by the Spanish painter ANTONIO CARNICERO, sent to the Editor by Enrique Morfin, Dr. Barragan 287 Mexico, 7, D.F.

Chapter 5
John Russian

The hogs we had been hunting throughout our area were all either descendants of the original Desoto Feral Boars, or Boars that farmers from the beginning of colonization until the 1970s had ran in the woods, and usually it was a mixture of both. But we did something in 1971 that would change that, we brought the first Russian Boar to the State of Mississippi. My Grandfather got with my cousin Johnny McCulloch, from Tennessee and asked for a Russian Pig from the smoky mountain area of Tennessee. Now Johnny bear and hog hunted in the mountains near Tellico Tennessee where the original Russians were brought in by Gordon Moore in 1912. Johnny was the man for the job, like everyone he loved and respected my Grandfather and would do anything for him. Soon he brought us a little Russian Boar pig, about a month old. We raised him in Grandma's back yard and called him John Russian. He grew to be a fine, long, lean, breeding machine, and my grandfather put him to use. Being a farmer all his young life in Tennessee before the War, Pa understood the value of good blood. He built a two acre hog pen at our home out in the country in Lizana Mississippi. He had two boys that were hog hunting up a storm in the early 70s and bringing them all home alive. He charged them with keeping that pen full of 80 to 100 wild sows at all times. The plan was to breed them all to John Russian, and when they were showing 'heavy bred' return them to the hog woods throughout the deep south.

Now this would be something that many other hog hunters, like Dennis Good of Slidell Louisiana, would do in the 80s, but we were the first by about 10 years. John Russian was the first Russian blood to flow from the Sabine River on the Louisiana / Texas border, to the swamps of Central Florida. After we started putting those bred sows in the woods, every litter of pigs you would find would have one or two that were striped like a chipmunk. It was beautiful, and each time we would see one, we would smile. In those first 10 years Daddy, Jack, and Pa put hogs in every patch of woods that they felt would be right to sustain a herd. We used to catch hundreds of hogs in those first few years and bring them all home alive. Everyone who knew the numbers we were leaving the woods with wanted to know what in the world we did with them all, well now you know the secret. With the help of John Russian, we were spreading the love, and trying to keep us plenty of places to hunt.

Now this infusion of Russian blood we believed would make these Feral type boars even tougher and more hardy for the woods. My Grandfather's breeding program with John Russian was based to that very idea. Now as an older man myself and looking back after a lifetime of hog hunting, I truly believe that that original Desoto Feral that filled the swamps of the South Eastern United States is the toughest damn animal on the planet. Today I have a Wild Boar Hunting Lodge and it has afforded me the opportunity to be associated with about every line of Wild Boar that North America has to offer. There are presently 5 different lines of European Boar in this country and while they are a stream lined and gorgeous animal, I do not place their toughness and resilience above that of a good, tough, solid Desoto Feral Boar. If I see a sow of these European lines have a litter of pigs, it will usually average numbering around 5 little ones, and of those five it will surprise me if 3 live. A Desoto Feral sow on the other hand will average having around 8 pigs in a litter and it usually surprises me if any of them die. My lifetimes experience has shown me that they are just a heartier animal.

As for the mature males, I like to tell people that if I see a sow in heat and a group of boars fighting over her, it will be a Desoto Feral that breeds her first. In combat, they are just simply tougher than the Europeans. At my present age of 51 years old, with a lifetime of dog hunting behind me, if I named my top 50 toughest boars I ever caught with dogs, not a single Russian, or European, would be on that list. That Desoto Feral has shown me time and time again to be just a flat out survivor. Looks like those wise explorers of old knew which animal to spread around the world.

Boars tend to grow a thick, grissel, shield on their shoulders as they mature. Now maturity on a Boar is much like that of a Deer, Bear, Elk, etc. it begins at about three years of age, and tops out at about five years old. Now this shield would remind a person of a cutting board like you would have in a kitchen to cut up vegetables on. It is a thick grissely type substance that grows just under the hair on a boar. It's purpose is for defense. When two boars fight, they usually face each other, positioning themselves with each ones head at about the shoulder of their opponent. They then begin slashing at one another's shoulder and rib area. This will continue until one hurts the other enough for one to break and run. The Boar who has the best shield can take a deeper cut without harming them, because until the other boar actually cuts all the way through this shield, his tush does not actually reach any muscle to cause blood or pain. Yes, that means that if a boar has a 2 1/2 inch thick shield, and his opponent cuts a 2 inch deep gash in his shoulder, it does not even cause the boar to bleed one drop of blood because the tush has not even reached actual meat or muscle. So the boar with the longest teeth, coupled with the best shield, wins the fight, gets the girl, and of course passes his good genes along to the pigs. So through natural selection in the woods, one can see how this fine 'shield trait' would be passed along. Of the best shields that I usually see they are on the Desoto Feral more often. Russians will grow them, but usually not nearly as thick as you will find on the Desotos.

Length of teeth however, I have found to be about the same, if not longer on the more Russian type boars. Now many good ole hog hunters have all types of theories on what makes teeth longer on a boar. Well allow me to explain to you just what determines the length of teeth on a boar. The two main top teeth, what we always called a whetter, is what sharpens the two main bottom teeth. What determines how long those two bottom teeth are is where the two top teeth are situated in their mouth. As those bottom teeth grow they curve back towards the hogs eyes. By doing this they then hit these whetters. The whetters made of a much harder substance than the bottom teeth, and when they meet, as the boar matures, they begin to rub off and sharpen the bottom teeth. This rubbing and sharpening will continue the boars entire life. Now the bottom teeth continue to grow every single day just like a fingernail. Each day they grow, and each day they sharpen off. This way if the boar were to break a bottom cutter in a fight, then over time by growing a little each day, then in a matter of a month or so it will grow right back up and sharpen right back off and he is ready for business again. Now when you realize how these teeth rub together and keep the bottoms sharpened to a certain length, then you have the ability to understand how some teeth get longer than others. If the top whetters, set in the usual place then normal teeth will sharpen off to about 2 1/2 inches long. But if the boar has a bit of an overbite, it will cause his whetters to set a little further forward in his mouth. This will cause the bottom teeth to be sharpened off to a much smaller length. I have seen six year old boars with bottom cutters being less than an inch in length, because the whetters set right up over the bottoms and simply cut them off shorter. On the other hand, if the boar has a bit of an underbite, then his whetters will set further back in his mouth, thus allowing the teeth to get longer than normal. Now from time to time you will see a boar whose skull is shaped in such a way, maybe due to an injury, that the bottom teeth actually miss the whetters entirely. In this case they just keep growing, like a fingernail. When reaching a certain length they will either break off and start again, or sometimes they will grow plum over and around and grow back into the boars skull, sometimes leading to his eventual death. I have heard many old Southern boys say that if you castrate a boar his teeth will get longer. Well not unless castrating him changes the configuration of his skull, causing him to have an underbite. What you are seeing with a castrated boar, is a boar that does not fight, so his teeth stay in a pristine state and at there maximum length. While a boar that fights for girls all the time usually keeps his teeth broken up, and always in a growing state to get back to maximum length.

Now the actual scoring system for boars is flawed to say the least. To score a boar, you remove the bottom tooth from the skull, measure its entire length, then take the circumference in the middle, and that is your score. See with those bottom teeth growing all the time like a fingernail it begins preparing to grow way back into the jaw bone. Which basically means that the bottom teeth have already developed and stick way back as far in the jaw as room will allow. This means the bigger the jaw, the longer these teeth grow back in there. This means that Russians and Desoto Ferals, which are the original wild hogs never hold the records with this style of scoring. All the top records are held by a more Domestic Boar, because they are much bigger, have bigger jaws, which allows for more teeth to develop back in the jaw bone. What makes it unfair is that Russians as a general rule have longer teeth growing out of there gums. Desoto Ferals are next as far as actual length from the gums. These monster domestic hogs tend to have the shortest actual length teeth out of the gums. My opinion is that only what sticks above the gums at the time of the kill should count. When you measure what is below the gum line and back in the jaw, you are not measuring what he has, you are measuring what he has in 'stand by' growth. I also believe that you should only measure him if he hits his whetters properly. This out of control growth that happens when a whetter is missed could break all records due to an injury or an abnormality in his skull. Fair scoring should be on a level playing field, but that is just my opinion.

Many do not know this, but the closest thing in the world that a wild boar is kin to is a bear. This can be seen in their movement and travel patterns. Boar and bear are the same. Females and young ones will range from 5 to 15 miles. A male will range out as far as 50 miles. Also you hear talk in hunting camps about how heavy boned a bear is, well a wild boar is actually heavier boned than a bear.

The thing however, that impresses me the most about hogs is how smart they are. I tell people that they are 'chimpanzee and dolphin' smart. I like to say that the only people who do not realize how smart a hog is are people who have never been around hogs. Not long ago there was a bit of a 'Potbelly Pig Craze' that went on. What amazed everyone who participated in the craze was how smart and easy to house train those pigs were. Most estimate that it takes days, if not weeks, to house train dogs and cats. Most agreed that the average time it took to house train a pig was about 4 hours. Another fine example came years ago in London England. See in many places in Europe they use hogs to find truff les. So someone came up with the idea to train a hog to be a drug sniffing animal. See a dog with an extremely good nose can smell through about 4 to 6 inches worth of soil, while the average hog can smell through 4 to 6 'feet' of soil. Instead of using a big domestic hog, they captured a small European pig. This pig was a sow, and they sent her to Germany to be trained by the top dog trainer in the World. After her training was over, her trainer said that she learned everything he taught on an average of four times faster than the very smartest dog that he had ever trained. This sow went on to become one of the most decorated drug animals in the history of the job, finding things in many cases that everyone agreed that no dog could have found. Now that of course, was due to her nose, but every officer that ever came in contact with her said that she was brilliant in every respect. Now a person could go on and on with such stories, but my experiences with their intelligence was in the woods.

We often hunted the Pearl River from about Bogalusa Louisiana south to where it spills into the gulf. We hunted mainly the Mississippi side further north, but when it gets down a ways it splits into East and West Pearl, and down there we hunted either side. Now again these big rivers in the deep south are all on very flat southern soil, so there is a flood zone area on each side of the river. This is where, in a good heavy rain, it will flood several times a year so building and populating these areas with houses is out of the question. So the State just writes them off as Wildlife Management Areas. These flood zones usually stretch out about an average of four miles on each side of these rivers. Well hunting is allowed in these areas, but only during the open hunting seasons. In the off seasons from hunting in the summer months the hogs spread out everywhere in the swamps. They can be found on the river banks, all the way across to the highways and roads that border the outskirts of the flood zones. These were the months that we loved to hunt the most in these swamps. Not only were the hogs everywhere, but there were no hunters in the woods, also the swamps were a lot drier in the summer due to less rain, and this allowed us to have a nice dry hunt that also allowed us to go everywhere. But when discussing a hogs intelligence, a cool thing happened in this swamp. Squirrel season was the first to open in our area. On the first day of squirrel season, every hog in the swamp would head into the deepest part of the swamp. In the summer hogs could be found the entire four miles wide of this flood zone and for the length of the river. As soon as the first shot of squirrel season sounded they all headed in. Now they could still be found for the entire length of the river, but not for a mile from the river bank, nor for a mile of the out lying roads. Basically for the remainder of all hunting seasons for the year they stayed within the two mile center of that flood zone like clock work. Most hunters don't have the sack to hike in a mile to begin to hunt. This helped us in the winter months because we did not want to be around other hunters either, so where we had to go to get to the hogs, was where we actually wanted to be as well.

Hunting Texas for hogs today also gives a perfect example of a hogs intelligence. Texas is on an extermination policy when it comes to hogs. They believe what they are spoon fed about hogs by the ever so reliable television set, so the goal is to shoot every hog they see. They believe that hogs are spreading and populations are increasing. They also believe that hogs will hurt their deer populations. This of course could not be further from the truth, every place that we tend to find the highest deer populations, we also tend to find the highest hog populations. They actually seem to complement each other. Oddly enough the entire State of Texas is the perfect example. The sections of the State that hogs populations are the lowest, deer populations are also the lowest, and where they are the highest for hogs, they are also the highest for deer. But most folks in Texas, and other Southern States for that matter, seem to miss that very obvious fact, and enjoy believing what they are spoon fed by the media. But due to this Texas extermination policy the hogs in that State go completely nocturnal after reaching a certain age. Nocturnal meaning they feed and move primarily at night. When someone tells me today that they have hunted hogs in Texas, I say, "Let me guess, you killed a 60 pound sow". Their response is always, "Yes, how did you know". Well it is simple, only very young hogs move about in daylight hours in a State like that. There are plenty of Trophy Boars in Texas, but without the use of dogs, you will never see him. My friends out there who, do not hunt with dogs, and zero in on a big boar with trail cameras tend to find that he leaves his hiding place where he beds up at about 2 am, and then returns to it about 4 am. This avoids the assassins slipping about in the daylight, but it also avoids those doing the night hunting as well because by 2 am they have usually headed for the comfort of a bed.

He is in truth an amazing foe. Hard to bay up in an area that is heavily hunted, tough on dogs once he is caught,hard to find when dogs are not being used, and he can survive anywhere. I have always felt that he is the single finest Trophy Big Game animal that North America has to offer. I have hunted all over the World and have taken Big Game animals from Africa to New Zealand, and none provide me with the challenges that a big mature boar can offer. Now our bringing John Russian into South Mississippi may not have increased the toughness of the Desoto Feral boars already in that area, but it did not hurt in any way their intelligence and cunning. Also the look of a good Russian Boar is hard to match. No Trophy Room in North America is complete without a good shoulder mount of a Wild Boar, and when it comes to the appearance of the boar as a trophy the Russian has a lot to contribute. The long straight snout is a classic Russian trait, along with the nice Razor Back hair that can be found on their winter coat. Now when talking about a Russian we are looking at a coat that is primarily either black or a very dark brown, with gold and /or silver accents primarily found around the head and mouth. But I have to admit that the wide variety of colors offered to the Trophy Hunter when he starts looking into the Desoto Feral Boar as a trophy option is unlimited. But all in all the mixture that my grandfather, with the help of his sons, created with John Russian in South Mississippi, Louisiana, and Alabama in the early 70s was a benefit to the wild boar in that area as a Big Game Trophy Animal.

We bred to and distributed pigs off of John Russian for around 8 years. We kept anywhere from 40 to 80 sows with him at all times. In many cases once they were bred we returned them to their original homes. Some we spread to places that we felt would be a good place for wild hogs. Others we allowed to pig at home and when the pigs were up about 40 to 60 pounds, then we would transplant them. John Russian was a fine Boar and died of a simple accident.He was bedded in the back of the field and Daddy walked up on him one day, he wasn't sneaking but John Russian did not hear him approach. When he finally did, it startled him. He jumped up, spun quickly, slipped and it crippled him. He had always been a big pet, the startling was not due to a fear of Daddy, it just surprised him. He stayed crippled, lost weight, and eventually died. Upon an autopsy done out of shear curiosity, we discovered that when he slipped it spit the hip bones where they connect between his legs. You know how when you gut a deer, between his legs the bones connect right where the tube to his annus connects to his guts. Most folks use a little saw to cut it. Well that split apart when he spun and slipped. It was a damn shame and the loss of a fine brood boar, but he had made a contribution to the Gulf Coast that, although most hog hunters in the area do not realize, can still be found today.

The mentioning of his death is a good spot to answer an often asked question about Wild Boar. Many times I have been asked how long a Wild Boar can live. Well the oldest living recorded Boar was in a zoo in Berlin Germany and he live to be 23 years old. Now that is not normal, it is the record, but keep in mind in a zoo he was receiving the finest care the world has to offer. Also this was in Germany, so he was receiving it from the smartest scientists in the world, but he did have a nice long life. I myself tell folks to think of it like a dog. We had a bulldog that lived to be 19 at one point. He produced pups until he was 17. As for hogs I have had several that lived to be 16 or 17 years of age, but on average the life span is usually 10 or 12. Again, just like a dog. So with that in mind you could use the old '7 dog years is the equivalent of 1 human year'. This is the calculation I also use on hogs.

This is a Head Mount of John Russian. This is the only big game animal that my grandfather ever paid to have mounted and it hung in my grandparents house until their deaths. John Russian was the first Russian, or European, Boar to be brought to the South Mississippi area. We spread his bloodline throughout the Deep South States from Texas to Florida for many years.

Chapter 6
Our Return to the Hog Woods

Due to a very low population of hogs after about an eight or so year onslaught by my father and uncle, also coupled with their getting more involved with another sport with the American Pit Bull Terrier, we laid completely off of hog hunting for a few years. Myself, I had been dying to get back to hog hunting, but being a kid I did not dictate policy in our household. But in the State of Mississippi in my day a young man could get his driver's license at the age of 15. So on the morning of my fifteenth birthday, I was sitting at the driver's license building when they opened. I had also been working with my father for a few years collecting his cull bulldogs where I could. The plan was to begin hog hunting on my own, if necessary as soon as I could drive myself to the hog woods. We had completely wiped out the hog populations within short distances of the house, so to get to any hogs it was a minimum of a 30 minute drive, and to get to the real river swamps, I was looking at an hour. Now from this point forward more accurate dates will be given and also you will notice more photographs. See to say my father and uncle cared nothing for Trophies of any kind is an understatement. Myself I at least began keeping a photo album with records and dates. From the age of 15 forward is where I became a real hog hunter.

Now the dogs I had collected from my father were all culls from his other dog occupation. There were several, but due to being involved in other things for a time to determine their value they could not be hunted together. Now of all these culls that I had collected a male named Jakel was by far the best. See Jakel was not a cull from other things because he was no good, like the others I had collected at this point, he was a cull because he had a breathing problem. A gamer finer dog did not exist on the earth than Jakel, but very long into combat and he would begin to show this breathing disorder. Well due to the nature of my father's other profession this just would not work, which made him perfect for me because he was as tough as a twenty penny nail and would charge straight into a Grizzly Bear, and when he caught him you would find out how loud a Grizzly Bear could holler.

I began hunting all the close places around the house with Jakel, but it was deadly dangerous. Those places were way too populated with farms and houses and Jakel would catch anything on the planet that moved, horses, cattle, dogs, anything, he was straight out insane. I loved him to death. I wanted to be in the River Swamps, but at my age mama did not want me ranging out that far. Then a stroke of luck hit me. Me, my Grandfather, and my cousin David Mitchell deer hunted together all the time. A Dog Man friend of my father's named JD Breland in-

Mitch Kemmer with Kemmer's Jakel. Jakel was off of Kemmer's Macho and Kemmer's Sissy. A gamer dog has never walked the earth and that statement comes from the hardest, coldest, man you will ever hear speak on the issue of gameness. It was a pleasure to have been able to have touched a dog like him.

vited us on a big deer hunt at his place in Beaumont Mississippi. We went up for the hunt, which in Mississippi was with dogs. During the day a pack of deer hounds ran up on a group of wild hogs, three of them, and the hogs ran the hounds out of the woods. The man making the drive saw the hogs and reported it to JD. Well when he told us about it, I went straight home and reported it to Daddy. He knew that I had been scalding the earth for a hog hunt, so the following weekend we took some of my grandfather's tough old cur dogs up there. With some direction from JD, who knew the area well, we found and caught all three hogs. Now this event did not spark an instant fire in my father to bound back into the hog woods, but it did cause a spark.

Another event in this time frame would also help lead my father back to the hog woods. Now as much as I was burning for him to get back into hog hunting with me, I can never refer to this event as lucky. A new dog disease appeared across the US, it was called Parvo. Today you think of it as something you simply vaccinate for, but back then it was new and it was horrible. We lost hundreds of dogs to it, primarily puppies under four months old. But it also, as we would learn, killed old dogs. It not only took out hundreds of prospective puppies of ours over a three year period before a vaccine came out, but it also killed our primary stud dog, a male called Macho. Macho was Jakel's daddy and the primary reason for Daddy's shift from hog hunting to another dog sport. This male was outstanding and with his pups, my father had dominated a certain dog sport for around 6 years. With the loss of Macho, and an entire section of our competition sport prospects due to the loss of all our young dogs, he fell into a lull period. Now he was still more active in this lull period in this other sport than most in that sport were in their busiest years, but it was a lull for him. He began to be willing to give up at least Saturday mornings for me. We began to hit the brush with Jakel.

Any single decent catch dog off of our bloodline of bulldogs could catch and hold any hog on the planet by himself, but Jakel was above average. Now at this point Jakel didn't even know what the hell a hog was. After 10 years of having our property completely saturated with hogs, during Daddy and Jack's hiatus from hog hunting we had not had a hog on the place for years, Jakel had never even seen one. You have to understand the Pit Bulldog's mind to understand this, but Jakel caught everything that moved, a frog, a bird, or a Brama Bull. Folks used to ask me, "How do you train a bulldog to catch?". My response was, "You don't. You train him what NOT to catch". Jakel was the prime example of that, but in his case we never could break him from catching anything. Our first successful trip to the woods with him for hogs was a trip to Rotten

Bayou near home. Daddy used to hunt there all the time but it was empty of hogs the last year that he had hunted. We began to hear rumors that a few hogs were beginning to build back up in there. So we took Jakel for a walk, straight up that Bayou. All of a sudden we rounded the corner and came face on into about 8 hogs. As soon as Jakel saw movement he nailed it. A nice young red and black spotted boar with a white blaze on his face. He was only about 80 pounds, but Jakel was a hog dog.

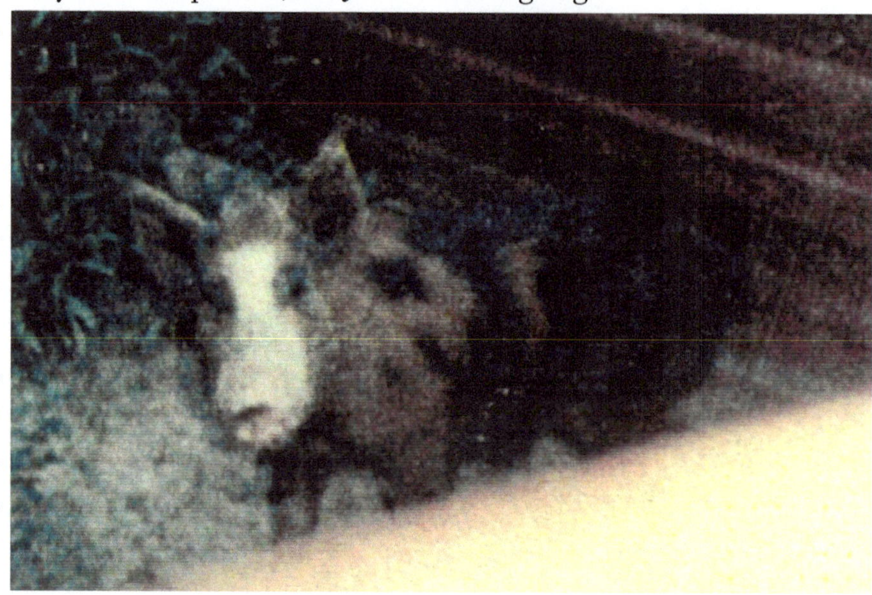

Jakel caught this Boar on Rotten Bayou in Mississippi. This was Jakel's first catch.

We soon began hitting the river swamps with him and catching hogs. Well he caught everything he saw, mink, fish in shallow pools, beaver, snakes, but yes we would usually get him on a hog. He did not have a nose at all, but Daddy and I were Navy Seal type trackers and if we found a hog track, and had enough daylight, we could usually end up getting Jakel in sight of him, and if he laid eyes on him there was no getting away. Jakel was far from a Hud or a Judge, but I never saw him miss a hog that he laid his eyes on. One day we were walking through the woods and a hawk came flying through real low. Now I usually carried about a four foot stick with me in the spring of the year in the swamp to knock down spider webs as I walked. As the hawk flew by I hit him with my stick and knocked him down just for fun. I then pinned him to the ground with my stick and took a picture of him. See I did such cool stuff my entire life that few people believed my stories. Well I brought a camera on a lot of our hog hunts so why not prove it. After taking the photo Jakel came running by, spotted the hawk and killed him, oh well.

This is the Hawk that I swatted down with a stick in the swamp as he flew by me. I used the stick to pen his leg while I pictured him.

Another day we were in the swamp with a High School Football buddy of mine CV Meadows. Daddy spotted an Owl in a tree and told CV that he could catch it. Not knowing my father, who could do anything by the way, CV laughed. Daddy slipped up to the tree that this Owl was 30 foot up in, Daddy then grabbed the small slender tree and gave it a good jerk. The tree warped the unsuspecting Owl in the head, knocking him senseless, and to the ground he fell. Daddy then caught him and we proceeded to take pictures of him. CV insisted on a photo of him holding the Owl. Upon handing the Owl to CV it grabbed his hand, CV then began to make this pain stricken face. I said, "CV you don't want a photo with you looking like a puss, man up for just a second while I snap this photo". He did and took a fine manly photo during that split second. Then we peeled the Owl's talons out of CV's skin and we released him. Luckily Jakel never laid his eyes on the Owl.

Then came our finest hunt with Jakel. It would have been the summer of 1984, between my Junior and Senior year of High School. We left the house at 5:30 in the morning, drove to the Bogalusa boat launch, took about a 40 minute boat ride then pulled the boat up in the woods to hide it. Game Warden's crawled up and down that river. We left the boat at 8 am and would not get back to it until exactly 8:30 pm that night. Jakel caught a fine mink that morning. The swamp was dry as a bone that summer so we could go anywhere we wanted. Being dry it caused all the little outlying pools of water

The first photo (above) is the Owl in the tree before we caught him. The second is Norman Kemmer holding him right after the catch. The third (above right) is CV Meadows getting his mind right for a photo. The Owl was then released.

and slues to dry up. That morning we found Gator tracks about a mile back in the swamp, whatever hole of water he had been in had dried up so he had to walk to the river. We all commented that we hoped Jakel didn't see him, or he would have been a caught Gator. What a picture that would have been. We walked all day. As I have stated before that TV propaganda about hog population explosions are people not living in the real world. Hogs were scarce, even deep in these river swamps, we hunted hard all day. About 3 pm we hit a waller with fresh sign in it. It had been a sow about 150 pounds, judging by the tracks, and she had fresh baby pigs with her. This was a sure fire score if we could stay on the tracks. Sows with very small pigs don't range far, but the swamp was dry, the ground was very hard, and tracking was tricky. Jakel couldn't trail at all so we had to get within sight of the hog for him to find it. Crawling on my hands and knees at times, looking for the slightest sign, it led me eventually to an old dried bed of a slue. As I followed the tracks down into the slue and up the other side I got a fine surprise. As the sow and her pigs tracks led into a good pig trail, a big monster track had joined them. In tracking situations such as these Daddy and I never spoke a word, we never broke a branch, we only gave hand signals. I then signaled back across the slue to Daddy as to what I had found. As we started following down the pig trail we could see a small 20 foot circle of briars just ahead. We stopped and scanned it because hogs love to bed in a thicket just like that. We heard a slight movement, looked and could see the boar standing in the thicket facing us. We looked for Jakel immediately and he had heard the slight sound as well and was facing the thicket at full alert. As the boar twitched Jakel broke for him like a rocket. The boar bolted out the back side of the thicket with Jakel right behind him. Watching a good intense catch dog run down an animal in an open swamp is a thing of beauty. From the moment Jakel laid eyes on him he was caught. As Jakel closed the distance he caught the first thing he came to and that was the Boar's ass. After slamming on the breaks and slowing the big 350+ pound boar, Jakel moved to the ribs for a grab, and then on to the ear. It was poetry in motion. As he hit the ear the big boar began his slashing. He flipped Jakel up over his head, slashing a big gash in his back leg. But know that the mighty Jakel was the kind of dog that could not be stopped until about 15 seconds after he was dead, and in the case of Jakel, I do not know that he would have stopped then. Daddy and I quickly caught up to them, me and a friend of mine Steve Stiglets, who had accompanied us that day, each grabbed a back leg as Daddy broke Jakel off the big boar. We then threw him on his side and tied him up. He was a caught hog.

Kemmer's Jakel with a 350+ pound Boar caught in Bogalusa Louisiana. Jakel was cut several times, but notice the large gash on his back hip. This Boar was whipping Jakel around over his head when I put my hand on his back foot. It was great, nothing like combat.

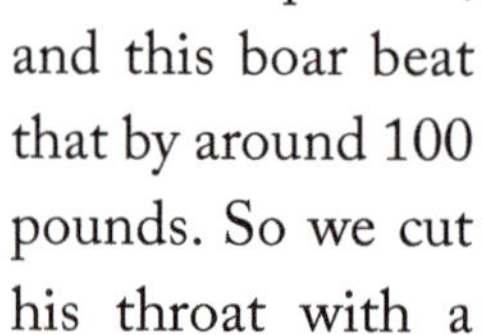

After the combat was over and the hog was tied we checked our watches and it was 4 pm. We were about 3 1/2 miles deep in the swamp, and this boar was bigger than we could carry on our shoulders alive. We could carry one out up to about 230 pounds, and this boar beat that by around 100 pounds. So we cut his throat with a pocket knife and began the trip out. Even dead weight and field dressed he would have been a struggle to get out with and make good time, so we cut him into three pieces.

One was his head, the other his two back legs together, and the third was his rib cage and front legs. There were three of use and the journey out that night was a long haul. The head was just an in the hands carry, but it alone weight 45 or 50 pounds. The two back legs were still together and were the easiest turn to take because you would just throw them over your shoulder and when you got tired you could switch to the other shoulder. It was the ribs and front legs that were the beast of the adventure. We cut two holes in the very back of the ribs for 'hand holts', then you put it on your head and allowed the front legs to drape over your back. We each took turns with every thing, but each man always had something. Again the ribs and shoulders were the worst. The top of your skull would be hitting the back bone on the inside of the ribs and most of the weight had to rest there. The bones, after a while, would dig into your skull. Daddy had worn a hat that day and we all began to wear it when it was our turn with that section. But on the very top of that damn hat was a little button type ball, as was on all baseball type hats in those days, and that was even rough on our already raw skulls. I never thought of Steve as a tough guy, but to his credit he toughed it right out. It was good for him, because my father had little patience for weakness. One of the things that I remember the most from my turns carrying that rib and front legs sections was that it was so heavy that when you grabbed the hand holts in the ribs and picked him up, you could not turn either hand holt loose for even a second or it would fall. As I would be carrying it big horse flies would land on my arms and begin

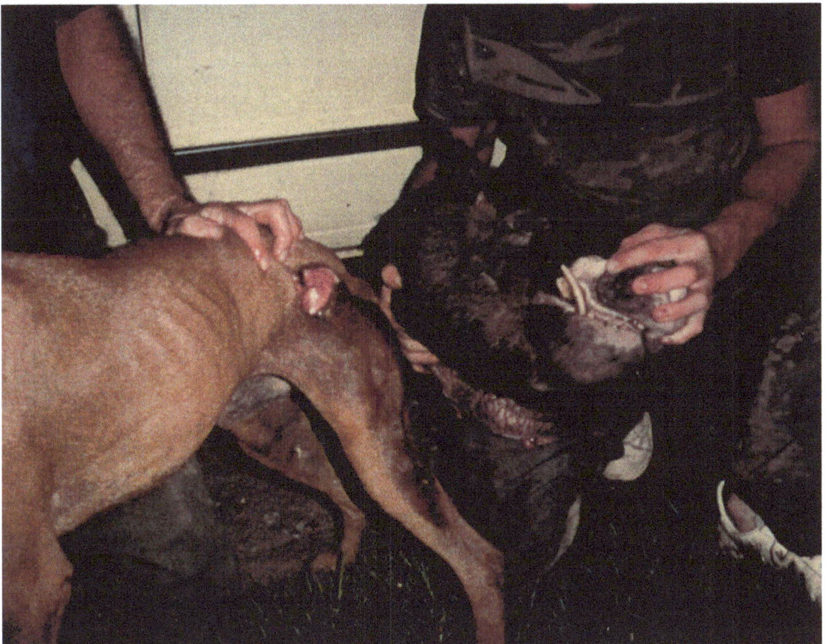

Norman Kemmer showing off Jakel's battle wound and Mitch Kemmer showing off a fine set of cutters.

biting me. Well because you couldn't turn loose of the hand holds, you had to leave them there until your carry turn was over. So you would watch them fill up and turn red with your blood, and as they filled up and dug in deeper in your arms they would turn almost straight out and instead of them just setting flat on your arm they would be out from your arm pointing straight in. It was the strangest thing to watch. When your carry was over and you would set the boar down the horse flies would be dug in so deep that it was like they could not turn loose. Then you just pulled them out of your arm. After that haul from the catch sight to the boat I counted 42 big purple knots on my arms where these big horse flies had been. It was a long day, a good hunt, one, as you can tell, that I have remembered all my life. I cannot recall a finer day. It is good to be tested. I heard a comment by a competitor in sports one time that said that few people in the world even knew what a 'second wind' was, because they never pushed themselves far enough to find one. We found our second wind that day, and our third, and are better men for it. Remember the Matilda speech……everything is a Battlefield.

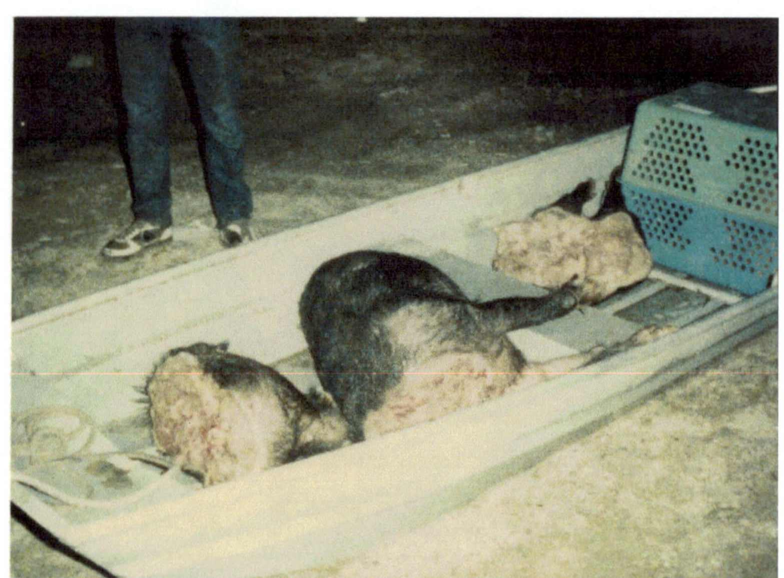

The Boar Jakel caught in Bogalusa was so big that he had to be cut into 3 pieces to make the long walk out that night. What a fine day.

We hunted Jakel several more times after that day catching two more hogs. Then we lost him one day in the very same woods where we had that fine hunt that day. Gator, hog, whatever, he was gone, and like the song in the movie Jeremiah Johnson, "He's up there still". He is missed by those who loved and respected him. If my theory of life is correct and God does hate a Coward, then he loves Jakel with all of his heart, as I did. The big boar that we caught in the swamp that day was a warrior himself. It was 1984 and he had an ear mark on him from the old 'ear marking' days before the stock law was passed. The stock law was passed in 1968, so this boar would have been more than 16 years of age. What a pleasure to see him and Jakel go head to head. What a fitting end for them both.

A head mount of the Boar Jakel caught in Bogalusa. I wanted you to see the notch in his right ear. This Boar was caught in the mid 80s and hog marking ended with the stock law being passed in 1968, so this shows the age of this fine Trophy.

A cool piece of luck came my way about this time. Daddy had reached a popular status in another dog sport, and a good friend of ours from West Texas, in that sport, came to pay us a visit. He had a friend with him from Japan. This Jap wanted to buy some dogs from my father. Now my father never sold dogs, especially good ones, but this Jap was after anything Norman Kemmer. Well I had a collection of four culls that I had been getting from Daddy over the years to hog hunt with. Daddy came to me and asked if he could sell that Jap my four dogs. Well Daddy had a black and white spotted male pup off a half brother to Jakel, bred to a super fine little female. This spotted pup that Daddy had was only about six months old but he had caught my eye since the day he was born. I offered to trade Daddy my four worthless dogs to sell to the Jap for this little pup. He agreed and this began my relationship with one of my very favorite catch dogs I would ever own. Not the best, but my favorite. His name was Speck.

Chapter 7
SPECK AND THE STORM

I would spend my life in association with the American Pit Bull Terrier in one sport or the other, and the good Lord saw fit to grace me with the perfect dogs for a specific sport that I was into at the time, on several different occasions. Now hog hunting is something I have been deeply involved in from my birth, I would venture to say, until my death, but Speck came into my life when I was not only in my absolute prime, but when I was at the very height of my interest in hog hunting. I got Speck when he was six months old and I was 17 years old. My Grandfather had helped me construct a hog pen when I was almost 15 years old. All of ours were gone from the old days, and when Pa saw me itching to hunt he helped me put together a good pen because by this time he fully understood what a determined person I was and he knew if I wanted to hog hunt......I would. I had several young boars collected in this pen that Jakel had caught. I took one out and put it in an acre field and cut Speck lose. Speck was by far the pick of his litter and had been on fire since birth. We had removed him from the pen with all his litter mates at 7 weeks old because he was killing them. The line of dogs that we had were far from normal, even for Pit Bulldogs. So of course, Speck nailed the boar like a seasoned pro. Now we have discussed different qualities in a catch dog. In hind site Speck would not become a Hud or a Judge, but he was damn close. He could trail way better than most bulldogs, he was extremely fast and tough as a pine knot. His only failing was that he was not a great snagger. He bobbled a little. Not bad, but over his life he did hit a few and they escaped. Jakel was good at snagging, if his hair touched a hair on that hog it was caught. Jakel was also fairly fast, but could not trail a hundred yards, he was more of a sight race dog, but nothing that he ever saw got away from him. Hud and Judge, of course, had it all.

Now the problem we had with Speck was one we often faced with our line of dogs, it was teaching him what not to catch. Now normally when we started them in the hog woods at this early age they were not hard to stop from catching the other dogs, Speck was different. He was bred for something way more serious than hog hunting and his pedigree showed through. His father Bo Bo, and his mother Widow were insanely perfect for this other sport, and Speck was his father and mother made over. Jakel could never be hunted around other dogs, he had gone way too far the other way to come back. Speck however was very young and I wanted to be able to hog hunt with him in any way I chose. We had been hunting with a bay dog or two over the last year. My grandfather always had cur dogs, and usually pretty rough ones. He had two at the time named Jim and LE. While we were hunting Jakel, we also had been doing a little hunting on the side with these two curs and a bulldog female that a friend of ours named Carl had, her name was Babe. She was a pure Pit, but was not off of our stuff, and believe me when I say that all pits are not created equal. Carl had an interest in bulldogs and had bought her before he met us. She was athletic and hunted well with other dogs because she was cold as the snow when it came to fighting. We had hunted with her for a time with the Jim and LE curs of Pa's.

The most interesting hunt we had with Babe, Jim, and LE, was the pursuit of a boar right off I-10 near the Mississippi Power plant off of Lorraine Road near the Gulfport and Biloxi line. We had heard reports of a lone boar traveling in this area and set out to catch him. Many local hog hunters had been after him and when we heard of his existence we took it as a personal challenge, if not an insult, that a boar felt he could set up camp that close to our house. Weekend after weekend we went after this boar. We always found sign and it was clear he was there for good, but we could never quite get on him. We finally decided to start baiting him with corn. He found the corn right off. Now when baiting with corn for hogs you have to understand that wide range they make. If they find corn on one day, then they will make their usual 5 or 10 or 30 mile swing that they range out, but the next time they find corn there they will remember it. This will cause them to range out a little shorter so that they can check this corn spot again sooner. If they find it then, then they check back even sooner the next time.

Before long they will realize that it is a consistent thing, and they will come every night. Now due to this initial procedure, you have to put it out every night. If he checks back and it is not there, then it throws off his process. Your consistency will guarantee his consistency. Once he gets on a nightly check, then he will set up camp in that area and have no need for the wide ranging hunt for food he normally does. That is how baiting works. So when we got him coming on a regular nightly basis, we began hitting that spot with dogs at all hours of the night. Now he was coming, but we never could figure out when. This was before the age of trail cameras. We were hunting old school. Well at this point we had been after this boar for over six months. We had never put this kind of time and effort into one hog. He was incredible, and we could not figure him out. Now when it came to issues like this we were as game as our catch dogs. The harder he was to find, the more determined we got.

Daddy and I worked together, he was a brick mason and I grew up working for him. Every day we would rattle our brains about how to defeat this enemy boar we were competing with. One day Daddy and I devised a plan based on something we had been told by an old Moonshiner in our area. He had told us that in the old days they would come into their 'Still Sights' early in the mornings and sometimes hogs would have hit the still. They would have gotten into the old sour mash corn. He said that the alcohol in the corn would cause the hogs to get drunk. They would then pass out drunk within a few feet of the still, and be laying right there when they arrived. After pondering this, we decided to buy some alcohol and begin soaking the corn with it before putting it out for bait. The plan was to get our opponent drunk, and even if it did not cause him to pass out, at least it might throw him off his game just a bit. The funny part was the trips to the liquor store. See Daddy, nor myself, ever drank in our lives, not ever. Neither of us had ever even tasted a beer. See Daddy never did, and he explained to me that drinking was a weakness, and that people did it because they could not face reality. Well when it was described to me as a sign of weakness.....well that was it, I knew I would never touch it because not only do I not have weaknesses, but I don't believe in them. So the liquor store visits were quite comical to he and I. But we had always heard of Jack Daniels, so that was our chosen weapon. We began soaking the corn for 24 hours in it before putting it out for bait. We baited for about a week, while not hitting the spot with dogs to give the juice time to take it's effect.

My cousin Dave Mitchell, future father in law, was in for a visit. He had became an Air Traffic Controller and had a life filled with moving from airport to bigger airports chasing promotions. But on all holidays he was at our house hunting with Pa, Daddy, Jack, or me. We asked him if he wanted to take a stab with us on this boar we had been pursuing for months. Like always he was all for it, and he must have been our good luck charm. Between him and the Jack Daniels, we got lucky about 11 pm that night. Jim and LE bayed the boar about 50 yards from the bait pile, Babe ran in on him and began to bay herself. What a worthless bitch. We had caught some young hogs with her to give her a taste, but this was her first run in with the real thing. Daddy and I recognized her bark right off the bat and we knew what was happening. Now we were finally on this boar we had been after for all this time and the only catch dog we had with us was a limp noodle. As we approached the sight the drunk boar was standing his ground and bayed up good and solid. Carl and a buddy of mine named Bryan Atwood (now a preacher in Gulfport) was with us. Daddy instructed the other three of them to surround the boars front and put lights in his eyes. He told me to bring my light around behind the boar with him. Then he told me to get down low and shine my light right on the boars left back leg. Daddy then slipped through the brush and caught the boar himself. We were not about to let this boar get away after all this time and effort just because we came to the woods with the wrong catch dog. I mentioned earlier on the Owl incident that my father could do anything, so of course you know he caught the hog. It was a long and fine adventure on this boar, but we realized that we needed a real catch dog off of

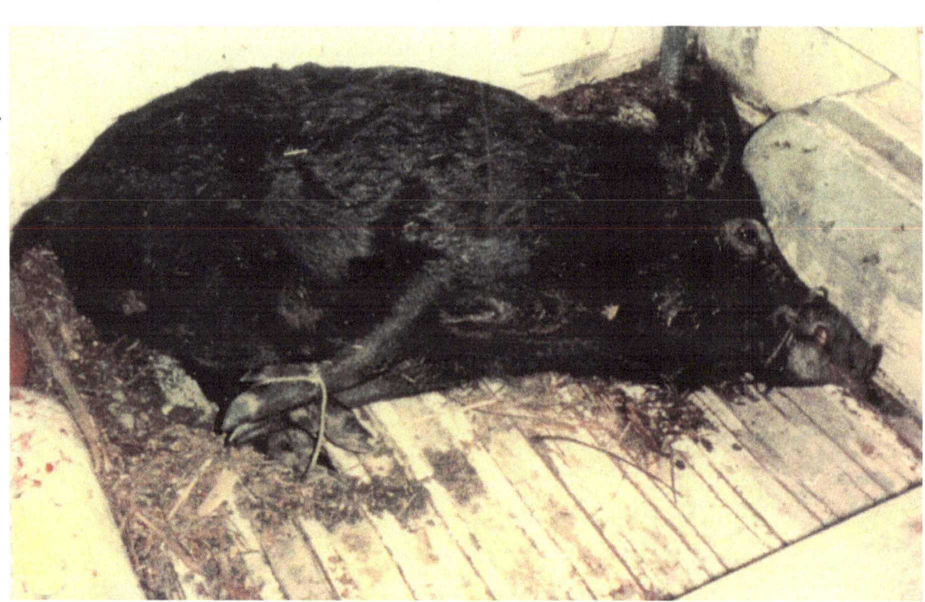

The illusive Boar from the Mississippi Power Plant near Loraine Road on I-10. Norman Kemmer had to catch this Boar, as the catch dog let us down. Normally it is females that throw a Trophy Male off his game, but in this case we used Jack Daniels.

our blood to hunt with these bay dogs. Well Speck fell into my hands within weeks of this incident.

Our first trip to the woods with Speck took place with the bay dogs Jim and LE. Carl was with us on that day and brought Babe. He had had her since she was a pup, and he was afflicted with something that my father and I never possessed, and something he would have to grow out of if he was going to hang with us. He had a weakness for her. He loved her. Now Daddy and I loved every dog we ever owned, as much as any man could love a dog, but once they betrayed us, like Babe had done on the 'I-10 Boar', it was time for the dirt nap. But anyway Babe came along. She proved to be very helpful that day in teaching Speck a life long lesson, and teaching me how much a dog could take and not die. I had Speck on a chain at first to lead him a while until he got a little used to being around other dogs. All he did was pull to get to them as I scolded him for doing so. Finally once we got deep into the woods, Daddy located a big stout stick and said, "Alright, turn him loose". Speck hit Babe, a 15 pound bigger fully mature dog, wide open. This six month old pup began wiping the ground with her. Daddy then began beating Speck with that stick unmercifully. Speck would not stop the full on attack, so we broke him off. We then tied Babe to a tree, backed Speck off, and released him again. The plan was to catch Speck coming in and work him over. Now first understand that to hunt him with other dogs he has to be broken from fighting, period, but also know that our theory on whipping dogs was our theory on whipping another man, kids, or anything. If the first whipping is severe enough, there will be no need for a second. Some parents, for example, do these little girly half ass whippings on their kids, and then they have to give a hundred of them in the kids childhood because the kid does not fear them. If you give the right caliber of whipping the first time, you will never be required to give a second one. Now some people might call it abuse. My theory is that one whipping is better than 100, and no whippings means no discipline, and that means the end of society as we know it. Now I had been a witness to many dog whippings given by my father, but none came close to what he did to Speck. Speck would not stop, no matter what he did. Daddy then grabbed Speck and tied him to a tree. He then sat down with me and we had a talk, as Speck was pulling desperately to get back to Babe. See Daddy was in another sport with the dogs, which I had also been raised around. Since the death of our Macho dog, Bo Bo's daddy, we had been getting less and less of the kinds of dogs needed for that activity. Daddy asked me to give him Speck back for that Sport, and let him give me something less in trade. Well

I had wanted Speck since he was born. It was his fire and gameness that I wanted in a hog dog. I had been dealing with plenty of culls around the time of Jakel and I hated a coward. Jakel was the real thing, but could not be hunted with other dogs. No.....I refused to trade him....I wanted a hog dog. After pleading with me, and my refusal, the beatings resumed. Once it got close to the point of death, Daddy gave me one last offer. I refused and on it went. He beat Speck so far down into the mud that his outline of his body could barely be seen. About 3 minutes after Speck stopped moving, Daddy stopped beating. I watched his body and rib cage for breathing, there was none, so I removed his collar an we all walked off. After we had walked about a mile, we looked back and here came Speck. Stove up and moving slow, he had pulled himself up out of the mud and trailed us up. I had never seen a beating to match the one he took. Not even close. Had he ever been allowed to fight, we would have never broken him. But starting that young, it was possible. As busted up as he was, we continued the hunt, and from that day forward he was a hog dog.

Now this hunt we were on this day was taking place in Diamond Head near the Pine Hills area. We had parked on the Pine Hills end and were working our way towards Diamond Head itself. We started getting into some hog sign and Jim and LE disappeared. Babe, and even stove up little Speck, began winding. The dogs all scattered out and we knew we were close. Then we heard Jim and LE bay, as we closed in closer we heard Babe arrive, it wasn't hard to know when she arrived because she started Baying as well. As we got into the thick stuff where they were Babe stopped baying. We did not know where the Speck pup was but with Babe's silence, we just assumed she had caught. The strange thing was that Jim and LE were still baying, which meant that the hog was not stable enough to them to catch. So we crawled in real slow and quiet. We got to where we could see a big, rangy, black Boar standing in front of Jim and LE, but there was no Babe on him or in sight. The brush was thick all around him, but as we got closer we saw something at the Boar's feet. It was little Speck. He was cut completely down, exhausted, and laying at the Boars feet and had his mouth on the Boar's front leg. He was caught. Once we saw him caught, we bolted in. The Boar jerked away from the exhausted, cut down, pup, and off he went. Speck got up and started after him, but we quickly caught him. We began looking for Babe, and about 10 foot from the bay sight, she was laying there dead. Her throat had been cut. He had hit a main artery, and she had bled out. We had heard her arrive and start baying, then she shut up. What we suspect, in hind sight, was that she was baying with Jim and LE, and when Speck arrived and actually caught the Boar, then the three 'bay dogs' moved in a little closer and the Boar got a good slashing cut at her. It was the only mark on her so it is doubtful that she ever actually caught herself. Anyway it got that worthless cur out of our hunting pack. Daddy and I hated hunting with people with worthless catch dogs. Hearing a bulldog bark in combat is not natural, so good riddance to Babe.

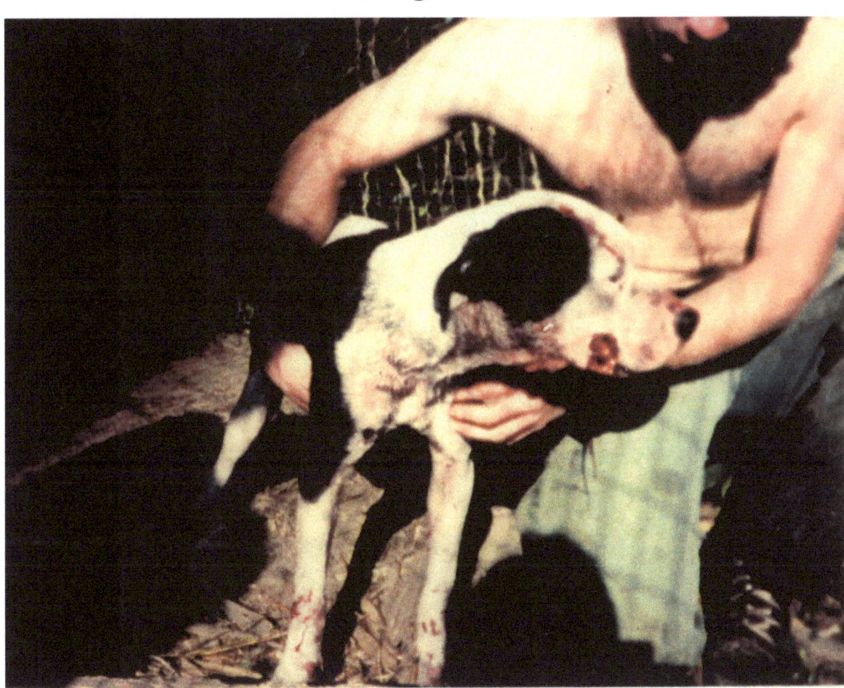

Mitch Kemmer and Speck. This photo was taken after Speck's first day in the hog woods. He received the beating of a lifetime to start his day and to end, he got cut to pieces by a big Boar that killed Babe.

Our next hunt with Speck would become South Mississippi Legend and we would not even catch a hog. Daddy had often hunted the Barrier Islands off the Coast of Mississippi, primarily Cat Island, Deer Island, and Horn Island. Deer Island in Biloxi was only about 1/4 of a mile off the Beach, Cat was about 4 to 6 miles out, and the Horn was about 12 or so miles out. Who ever had owned the Horn in the old days had put a bunch of Poland China colored black and white hogs out there. They had the thickest legs you could imagine on them. Daddy had been hunting out there for years. Him and Wayne Parker went out there one day. They pulled the boat up on the beach and took a short walk. There was an old Artesian Well out there. A pipe sticking up out of the ground about three feet that constantly spewed fresh water up out of it. They had walked about three hundred yards from the boat to get a drink of this water. After drinking from the well, Wayne looked back and saw the boat about a 1/4 of a mile in the ocean and leaving fast. Now if it had been two normal men on that Island they would have been stranded. Normal men can't swim and catch a moving boat that has 1/4 of mile head start in the open ocean, but my father was not normal. Ask Wayne Parker, he is still alive. Knowing they were doomed, in an age without cell phones and being on an Island that nobody frequented, Daddy headed out and caught the boat. Now this was the most famous Horn Island story up until the hunt I am about to speak of.

We awoke one Saturday morning and began to plan our hunt for the day. A friend of mine who hunted with us often named Greg Murray had spent the night with me. Now a Hurricane had been bumping around out in the Gulf for a few days named Elena. It was only a category 3 or so at the time, nothing to stop a hog hunt. We had been wanting to go to the Horn for a while, but with this Hurricane out there we were thinking more along the lines of a Bogalusa trip. So we woke early that morning and began to watch the weather channel. They had called for a Mississippi land fall for days, but as we watched that morning they were changing their story. The storm had taken an about face in the night and at 5:30 in the morning they were predicting a land fall that evening in South Florida. That cleared us to head to the Horn. Now Daddy's old work truck did not have a radio, so once we left the house we had lost all weather communication. We launched the boat at a harbor in Biloxi on the beach just in from Deer Island. The weather was calm that morning, exceptionally calm (calm before the s———). We did not have any big fancy boats at my house, we hunted out of a 14 foot skiff with an old 20 horse power mercury motor that Daddy and Jack had bought in 1968. This hunt was in around 1985.

As we hit the Island we got us a good drink from the Artesian Well and began our day. Horn Island had been purchased by the State and they had turned it into a Red Wolf restoration area. Red Wolves had nearly gone extinct as a breed, they had been cross breeding with Coyotes and the pure Red Wolf was almost a thing of the past. Horn Island, being isolated from the mainland was the perfect place, and the State had been trapping the purest of the pure Red Wolfs and also getting them from Zoos and releasing them on the Island to maintain the breed. Now we were not interested in Red Wolfs and luckily for them Speck never saw one, we were after hogs. But since the Government had taken control of Horn Island we were being extra cautious in our usual stealthy Navy Seal mode. As we hunted on into the day we began hearing extra boat traffic around the Island, we also saw a Helicopter scalding the Island pretty hard. We figured that they might be on to us, but you have to understand that no one caught me and my father when we were in the woods. When we noticed what appeared to be a search for us we just made it a point to become more illusive. Now 'bless their little hearts' but they were not going to find us. The hunt went on all day, we could not find hog sign one no matter how much ground we covered. We got back to the boat around dark and Daddy suggested that we just spend the night and hunt again the next day. Then my buddy Greg informed me that his Daddy would freak out if he did not come home that night. Well that sent my Daddy into a rage. Greg's Daddy Danny had hunted with my father years earlier and Daddy didn't really care for his ways. Also Daddy did not like anyone going hunting with us, and then causing us to cut a hunt short over them. It was his favor to them to allow someone to come along with us, and then they want to pay back the favor by screwing up our hunt. So Daddy through a fit for a few minutes and I began unpacking the boat to spend the night. Daddy then through his arms in the air and said, "Screw it, let's go in". So we left Horn Island for the shore line just as it was getting dark.

Mitch Kemmer took this picture on Horn Island on the day Hurricane Elena hit the Coast. The Horn is 12 miles out in the Gulf of Mexico. This photo shows Speck on the left, Norman Kemmer in the center, and Greg Murry on the right. Notice what a fine day it was that morning.

Now as an adult I have looked back on many of the things that I have been through as a red blooded american southern boy, and wondered how I lived through them. Well few more than this boat ride. As we pulled off of the Island it was getting dark and the wind and waves had begun to pick up. We had made plenty of trips in from the Horn after dark. Once the lights come on on shore you can keep your bearings, and once you get closer to shore you can see familiar things that get you near the boat launch. But tonight was different. When we got about a half a mile off the Island it got rough. Now for men like me and my father, what is rough to most is a joke to us, but this was rough to us. Not normal rough, it was real rough. Waves were so high we could not see the lights of the shore until being picked up and the boat slung higher up than the waves. Remember we are in a 14 foot skiff. I had on a Poncho that we kept for rain, and Speck was between my legs under the poncho, but soon the boat began to fill with water. Not a leak, but water from the waves. Daddy was steady on the motor. Normally you keep the boat turned into bad waves, but there was none of that. Waves rolled in from all directions. It was like we were in a bowl of water and it was being tossed straight up. Waves seemed not to have a consistent direction, so Daddy just kept her steady towards the Coast. Greg and I began bailing water out with anything we could find, mostly our hands. Fish were consistently jumping in the boat. A mullet hit Greg right in the head. Looking back on it all I do not know how Daddy kept that consistent speed and direction on that trip. It took us six and a half hours to get in and Daddy was like a statue, never losing focus, never changing speed, never swaying to one side or the other, and never taking his right hand off the Boat Motor. His toughness always impressed me. Every kid likes to think of his father as a superhero, well partner.....mine was, and anyone who knew him would attest to that. What a fine mentor, and what a tough tough man. No matter where I ever went with him, I always felt safe. This night was no different. I knew we were going home.

As we neared the launch, we came in between Deer Island and the coast to get to the launch. As we neared this gap between the Island and the Coast the waves were not nearly as big, because the Island was breaking the force. Daddy then let off the throttle just bit. The motor on that old 20 horsepower mercury then died........it never started again. It had been kept steady since the Island, but when he let off just a bit that was it. If Daddy had let off just 100 yards out, even to switch hands out of weakness, we would have had no motor. God hates weakness and he hates a Coward. That supreme toughness of my father and his ability to go six and a half hours with a steady pull on that throttle that night apparently saved our lives. It is apparent that God loves gameness as much as me, for he allowed us to get in between Deer Island and the Coast. We paddled in from there.

Now this rough weather up until this point in the night was bad, but we did not know what was really up with it until we arrived at the boat launch. As we pulled up to the pier at the launch my uncle Jack was there and so was Greg Murray's Daddy Danny. This seemed a little odd. Danny told Greg to get in the truck, which he did, and they both drove off without saying another word. Jack proceeded at that point to inform us that within an hour of us leaving the house that morning that Hurricane Elena had made an about face and had headed straight for the Mississippi Gulf Coast. When Greg's dad realized it he called mama. Well normally mama was not allowed to tell a soul where we were hunting, but being a woman she became as frantic as Danny once she realized that we were 12 miles out in the Gulf of Mexico and a major Hurricane was headed our way, and she also knew that we didn't know it. So with the two women, Danny and my mother, in a panic the days fiasco on the main land had begun. Danny had some political pull on the Coast and by mid morning was on the phone with the Governor of the State. He proceeded to tell everyone where we were and also he said, "They are on the Island and are illegally hog hunting and they will be hiding from you". So this explained the extra heat on the Island from the authorities. We thought they were trying to protect a few worthless wolves, but in truth they had the goods on us and were told by the Governor himself to catch us. Ha, fat chance of that. Now the reason that Jack and Danny were at the boat launch is because when the authorities could not find us, Danny had personally hired a helicopter pilot to fly him out to look for us, and they were waiting there for him to arrive. Now Jack wasn't worried about me and Daddy at all, he knew us well and he knew that only old age could kill us. No Jack had come for a personal reason. See Danny was known State wide to be a bit of an asshole, and Jack knew from personal experience that Daddy didn't like Danny. Now Jack had spent the entire day with Mama and Danny and had heard Danny cuss Daddy and talk tough about what he was going to do when he saw Daddy. Knowing my father, Jack knew that was a joke, but it was a joke he wanted to see played out. So along for the ride he went. He was going to get a free Helicopter ride in the middle of a Hurricane which promised to be interesting, and he said he wanted to be there when Danny saw Daddy. So the night turned out to be a big disappointment for Jack. We got back before the Helicopter arrived and Danny, of course, never said one word to my father.

The bulk of the Hurricane was hitting the Island about the time we got the boat loaded. Folks who aren't used to Hurricanes make a lot more out of them than they are. A real southerner barely misses work for anything less than a Category 3, and we never miss a hunt. Hurricane Elena hit the Horn as a Category 3 and, it was reported that it cut Horn Island into three different pieces. Folks often asked us what we would have done if we had spent the night and not boated in. Daddy always said, "We would have tied ourselves to a few trees and rode it out". Later the name Elena was retired from the cycle list of Atlantic Hurricane names because of the storm's horrible effects. This storm holds the record for causing the most wide spread evacuations in peace time in American History, due to it's bouncing around the gulf, heading one way, then the other. We had simply been a victim of it unpredictability. All in all it did make for a good story. Most people lead dull meaningless lives, I have always thought of them as sheep. I went to a Whitetail Deer hunting camp one time in Pachuta Mississippi. The owner of the place asked each hunter in camp to tell their single most exciting hunting story. There were ten people in camp that weekend and after listening to each hunter's most exciting story that they had ever had I came back to Gulfport and told my father that they made me realize just how lucky I was. Even the most exciting story of the ten was an event that, had it happened to me and my father on one of our hunts, it was so dull that we would not have remembered it by the time we got home. The 'Horn Island in the Hurricane' story would not be one of our best, but I do remember it. By the way, Greg's Daddy never allowed him to hunt with us again.

Chapter 8
Speck and Slim in Mobile

Our next challenge was finding another catch dog to hunt with Speck. A good catch dog, like Jakel, can catch any hog in the woods completely by himself, but two is better. It is better because with a dog on each ear, for example, the boar doesn't have the freedom to use his athletic ability, provided he has any, to get a good swinging slash or stick on a single dog. The two together basically anchor him more. Also we have had many dogs killed before we could get to the battle site, so with two dogs that still leaves one alive so that we can get our hands on the hog. Once we touch that back foot, it's all over. Then if one dog does get killed, we can still hunt the next weekend because we have a dog left over and we never miss a beat. You have to understand that all catch dogs eventually get killed, it's just a matter of when. We only retired one catch dog in our lifetime of hog hunting. We retired old Hombre. Hombre was the half boxer, half Pit that was our second catch dog we started after Hud. We retired him after he caught 304 hogs. But he would have eventually gotten killed I am sure if we had not retired him early. His early retirement was due to the fact that....well....he was a grouchy old Bastard. Even when he was young he was the type of dog that bowed up at everything that walked by him, that was the boxer in him. If a bulldog wants to fight, he just attacks you, no bluster and tough posturing, he just attacks. If you see a pure pit bulldog that does that old bowing up, raising his hair up, his tail bushing up, then that bulldog is a straight cur, or coward. Real true bulldogs are like a real tough man, no fluff, no big talk, just action. If we had ten dogs in the woods and one started that old bowing up and growling and starting trouble it was always one of the bay dogs. Of course that is the dog in the woods with the least potential to be able to back it up, but he starts it with that cur ass big talking nature of his. The boxer in Hombre made him that way. A fight is the worst thing to screw up a good days hunt. Once a fight has happened all the dogs are on edge the rest of the day, and only a slight bump can fire it up again. Hombre was fine if we were into hogs, but as the stock law days ended and hogs thinned out, he got worse. Boredom in the woods would cause him to begin his grouchy posturing and eventually a real dog would proceed to whip his ass, and the whole day was shot. The older he got, the worse he got, so we stopped hunting him long before we would have. Hombre died of old age at our house. So finding a catch dog with the right temperament to go with Speck was our plan.

Daddy picked a dog named Slim. Jackel was off of Macho and a bitch called Sissy. We were now breeding to Speck's daddy, a male called Bo Bo who was off of Macho. Well Slim was off of Bo Bo and Sissy. Dogs are like people; all have different demeanors and natures. Slim was a meek and docile acting dog, but caught good and real tough. All in all looking back on his life with us, he could not trail worth a damn, he was very slow, but he could really snag. Basically all the areas that Speck was strong in Slim was weak in, and Speck's weakness was Slim's strength, so they complimented each other. Many days I would out run Slim to the battle site, Speck of course would already be there, and I would wait for Slim to arrive out of fear that Speck might bobble his hold as I approached. Once Slim arrived I bolted in with all the confidence in the world. Slim never touched a hog and it get away. They were the perfect team and we caught many hogs with them. In a lifetime of hog hunting, I would see my 'high water mark' in hog hunting fun with these two dogs.

We began hitting these woods with our new team and snagging hogs here and there. Populations had rebounded a bit from the point when Daddy and Jack left for another sport, but these new populations were fragile. We knew from the old days that if we laid into a spot too hard we would wipe the numbers completely out, so we began a system. We hunted a few old reliable places that still possessed some hogs, and we began to check every rumor of a hog, and we developed about 20 places to hunt. Then we, very methodically, would rotate our hunting as to never over hunt particular spots. After catching 20 or so hogs with our new team, we lost our bay dog Jim hunting in the

Pascagoula River swamp one day. We feel certain that someone shot him. That is not a charge we make lightly, and of course we did not find the culpret or we would have killed him and I would omit this story from the book. But dog hunters face that reality every time they hit the woods, and we believe this is what happened to Jim. So LE was now the one bay dog, with Speck and Slim as catch dogs.

LE would turn into the second best bay dog we would ever own. Blackie was a 10 and LE was a 5, but we had settled on the fact that Blackie had set the bar so high that we took what we could get and 5 it was. LE had come to us by way of my grandfather who had gotten him as a pup from an old football and hunting buddy of Daddy's in high school, his name was LE Parker. He was Wayne Parker's cousin. LE was one of the guys that Daddy took with him to get the Red Gap Boar out of the woods after he killed Heck and Little Hud. But LE the dog had many things about him that I grew to love more than Blackie. LE did not range out how ever far it took to find a hog, he was a close range hunting dog so this allowed us to dictate the direction of the hunt. As a matter of fact LE was plum lazy, and stayed under our feet out of a fear of being ambushed by bulldogs, with which he would have some 'bad experiences' with over the years. Although he stayed under your feet it became apparent to us over the years that if he was under our feet, there were no hogs near by. If you looked and he was gone, it was time to get set, and boy Speck and Slim zeroed in on that fact after a while. They watched LE like a hawk and when he disappeared they got still, quiet, and on full alert. They both would stand like statues and listen for him. Everyone who knows me knows that I want anything I do, or touch, to work like a 'well oiled machine'. Well if I could pick three words to describe the team of LE, Speck, and Slim, and what they would turn into, those words would simply be 'well oiled machine'. They got to the point where we believed they were reading each others minds, Daddy and I joined right in. They were like Blackie and Hud, they spoiled me and after them no other team of dogs ever suited me because I knew what it was supposed to be like. They would become poetry in motion.

Now this time frame would see us hook up with a guy in Citranel Alabama. His name was Larry Biggs and we connected with him through a cousin of Carls who worked with him. Larry owned a hunting camp just north of Mobile Bay. Two Rivers in Alabama spill into Mobile Bay and just north of the bay they have some canals cut in between these rivers. This caused several Island type situations in this area and Larry's camp was on one of those. I never saw more Alligators in one place in my entire life than here. When I was young Alligator hunting in Mississippi and Alabama was forbidden because the Game and Fish Commissions in both States said that population numbers were too low there to warrant hunting and that gators in both States were endangered. Well them dumb bastards never hunted here. There were enough gators here to fill four States, but it was also eat slap up with hogs and deer.

Our first trip to this Alabama destination was on December 26, 1985. The high temperature that day was 6 degrees, and take note that is 6 degrees in the deep south, which means it is a wet cold that clothes will not keep out. It is cold to the bone, and this day would become a test of men. When we arrived at Larry's place there were six guys waiting there to go with us. All with their thick clothes and their fancy water proof boots on, and we chuckled inside because we knew what this type of hog hunting was like. Me, Daddy and Carl all wore nothing but tennis shoes. You see this type of hunting causes you to go into the water often and once a waterproof boot gets water on the inside, that nice waterproofness keeps it on the inside. Tennis shoes allow the water to come in and go out. A big pair of boots will drown a feller if the dogs swim a half a mile across river and you have to go after them. Now we sure missed our thick wooly hunting clothes on that 45 minute boat ride that morning but as the action got hot that day we were all three happy to be mobile and agile. These Islands, we would come to find, were just big Palmetto thickets that were mud from your ankles to over your heads. It was the only place I ever hunted in my life that had 'quick sand'. In short this was a place that in a fast paced all day hunt would separate the men from the boys, and this day provided just that type of action. We put our foot in the hog woods at 6 am that morning and loaded out that night and left the hog woods at 5 pm, and it was straight action and dog chasing all day. After three hours of action that morning our 6 hunting companions had reduced there worthless cur selves to riding up and down the river in their boats just trying to keep up with our pace, and pick up hogs as we drug them out to the bank. It was a man's day, a man's environment, a man's temperatures, and on that day there were only 3 men there. We broke ice with every step from daylight till dark, and 2 minutes after stepping in a spot it would freeze back. God hates a Coward.

On the first bay of the morning LE bayed a group of about six hogs. As the bulldogs passed me and rushed in I bolted forward to assist them. As I was running a Palmetto Reed went straight up my nose and I felt the needle on the end of it hit the corner of my right eye. Now not only does a Palmetto Reed have a needle point, but it has saw like briers on each edge of it, and it started a steady stream of blood that would last for six solid hours. I have spent most of my life bleeding from one form of combat to another, but this Palmetto Reed incident of this day would top them all. I do not believe in weakness, nor do I possess it, but a feller only has so much of that stuff in him at any one time and at the end of that six hours when the bleeding finally stopped I had begun to wonder if I was reaching my limit. When Daddy and the guys arrived at the battle site I had the hog caught and blood was already flowing into my shoe. Every step I took for the next few hours saw frozen blood flaking off of me. Those 5 powder puffs were begging me to go to the hospital, but Daddy and Carl knew me better than that, so they never said a word. Many good catches that day but the best one happened right at dark. We got to the boat and was loading catch dogs. We looked around and LE was gone. That only meant one thing so the listening began. As the wind laid for the evening we could hear him about a mile and a half in. As we arrived Speck and Slim had the big boar caught. Slim was under him and we could not even see him, he was buried so far under the mud I do not know how he did not suffocate, but we knew where he was by the dark blood bubbling up through the mud. It was by far the worst I would ever see Slim injured until his death. That boar had zeroed in on him and really broke him down. But caught he was.

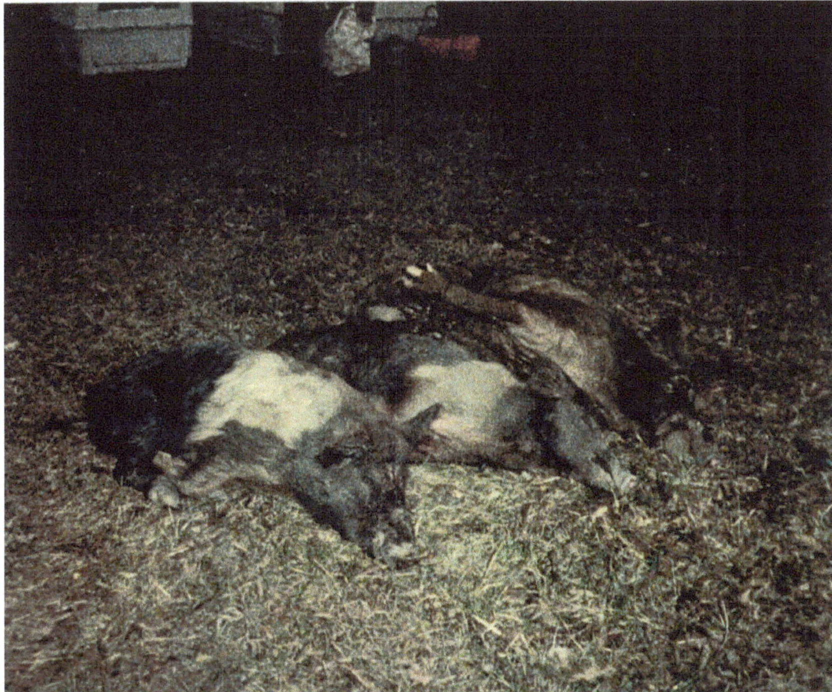

December 16,1985 with a high that day of 6 degrees. This was our first hunt with Larry Biggs and his crew in Mobile. The photo shows three of our catches on that day. To the far right is the big Boar that cut Slim all to pieces right at dark.

The boat ride out that night was one I would never forget. Shakespeare said, "A coward dies many times before his death. The valiant never taste of death but once". When a man quits, or admits that someone else is tougher than he is, he dies a little in that admittance. In fact he dies a little every day that he lives knowing that he is a coward deep down. A man like my father, for example, who has never stuped nor bowed will only taste death at the very end of his life. As we rode out that night Carl was setting on the front of the boat facing me, I was in the middle of the boat facing him, and our arms were both folded and both our legs were leaning up on the big boar we had just conquered. We knew we had not only done a man's days worth of hunting, but we had curred 6 men out that day. As we looked at each other that night on that cold 45 minute boat ride home, we both smiled at each other, and I said, "Man it don't get no better than this". Looking back on it now, thirty three years later......I was right.

Our next trip to Larry's place provided an interesting story about how well trained our dogs were. We had hit the woods and not long into the hunt Larry and his crew were actually still in the woods with us. Now Larry actually had a pack of dogs, if you want to call it that. Mostly they just fumbled around the woods aimlessly and obstructed our ability to hear LE when he bayed. Larry had a big old half English cloddy catch dog named Fleas. Well we were hunting down the edge of the river and I heard a boat going suspiciously slow. I motioned quietly to Daddy. When our dogs saw me motion to Daddy they all stopped moving and stood at alert. I slipped to the rivers edge and got where I could see. It was a Game Warden in a Patrol type boat cruising about 10 foot off the river bank look-

Norman Kemmer and Slim two days after the first Mobile Hunt.

ing intently in our direction as he eased down the river. I then spun slowly and put both hands out and motioned for everyone to squat down as I slowly squatted myself. Daddy, Carl, LE, Speck, and Slim all froze and squatted slowly with me. Genius Larry and his crew all stayed standing with this clueless look on their faces as their dogs continuously busted down brush ambling all over the place. Luckily the Game Warden did not see them as he moved on down the rivers edge. When Larry became conscious of what had just happened, he said, "Damn you boys are not only trained poachers, but you have poachers dogs as well". He was right the dogs preformed like a stealthy charm.

Later that day we ended up on another big bad boar in that Palmetto Mud Bog. I got to him first and caught the hog. As Daddy arrived and broke Speck off he realized that his throat had been cut several times. This was before the age of kevlar vests and collars. We immediately got Speck way away from the action to get him calm, applying pressure to his throat the entire time. I do not know how exactly he lived that day, blood was gushing, he bleed down and passed completely out, but he never died. I have never seen another dog live through a throat wound like that before or since, but he lived. We eased him out of the woods slowly and calmly, and he hunted the following weekend.

Mitch Kemmer and Speck two days after the first Mobile Hunt.

In another trip to this same Mobile area Daddy got cut by a big boar. Now our family was no stranger to being sliced by hogs. Dave Mitchell, was hunting with Daddy and Jack one day as a Boar got loose and spun on him. Dave with no time to prepare for the attack simply stuck both of his hands out in front of him as to push the boar away. The Boar bit his hand, just as the dogs caught him. The bite cut some tendons in Dave's hand that led to his little finger. Even after surgery, the finger was useless. Later in life he simply had it removed. Now Daddy and Jack teased Dave for a good while about sticking his hands out like that to receive a charge. They picked at him about that response for about a year until Daddy had a similar incident happen to him at home while we were cutting a boar loose. Usually when a boar has been tied all day, when you first cut the tie string off his feet he is slow to get up, but not this day. The boar hopped up, spun towards Daddy, and charged. Daddy immediately stuck both hands out in the same manor as Dave had done. The picking on Dave was over. Daddy later said that it was just the first reflex in that situation. The boar sliced Daddy's hand right between the thumb and index finger. Now apparently there is a damn fine artery in there because blood began squirting up about 4 foot with every heartbeat. As Daddy ran for grandma's house, she said she could see blood squirting with every step. They rushed him to the hospital and a young doctor sewed up the wound. About midnight that night Daddy woke up in excruciating pain. Now when Daddy said it hurt, everyone that knew him knew it really hurt. As they arrived back at the emergency room an old doctor approached and got the story. He then said in a furious voice, "You never sew up an animal bite". As he removed the stitches Daddy immediately felt the relief.

When we made this trip to Mobile when Daddy got cut again it was a simple mistake. When you have hunted as long as we have, you know what to do, and what not to do, but sometimes you just get careless. We had had a good day of hog catching and then LE bayed. I got there first and caught the hog. As Daddy arrived and began breaking off the dogs, Speck was caught under the bottom jaw. As Daddy grabbed his collar to break him off it put his hand right at the boars teeth. A quick slice and he was cut. He went on and broke Speck off and tied him. After we got the hog tied we inspected the wound. It was right over his old scar from his cut from years earlier, but it was not squirting blood. As we looked down in the wound we could actually see the pretty little blue artery that had been cut years before. Daddy wrapped a piece of cloth around the area and we continued hunting. I was walking behind Daddy and soon noticed a blood trail. The more we walked the bigger it got. I pointed it out to Daddy and we reinspected the wound. Apparently the hog had just nicked the artery and it burst open. The blood was really coming now. We worked Daddy to the river and sat him down. Carl went for the boat as I waited with Daddy. He told me that he believed that the bleeding had stopped. He was sitting on a stump and had his fore arm and hand resting on his leg. As the boat arrived and Daddy stood up we realized that the bleeding had not stopped. It had been running down the inside of his leg as we sat there and we did not see it. As he stood we saw a big pile of coagulated blood at the heal of Daddy's foot. On the long boat ride out he bled the floor of the boat full of blood. When we reached the truck we put a 5 gallon bucket between his legs and he bled about an inch and a half of blood in the bottom of that bucket. Upon reaching the house he refused to go to the doctor, knowing that sewing it was out of the question. But I will say this, after that day I now know how much a man can bleed and not die. He turned white as a sheet, but was hog hunting the next weekend, just like Speck.

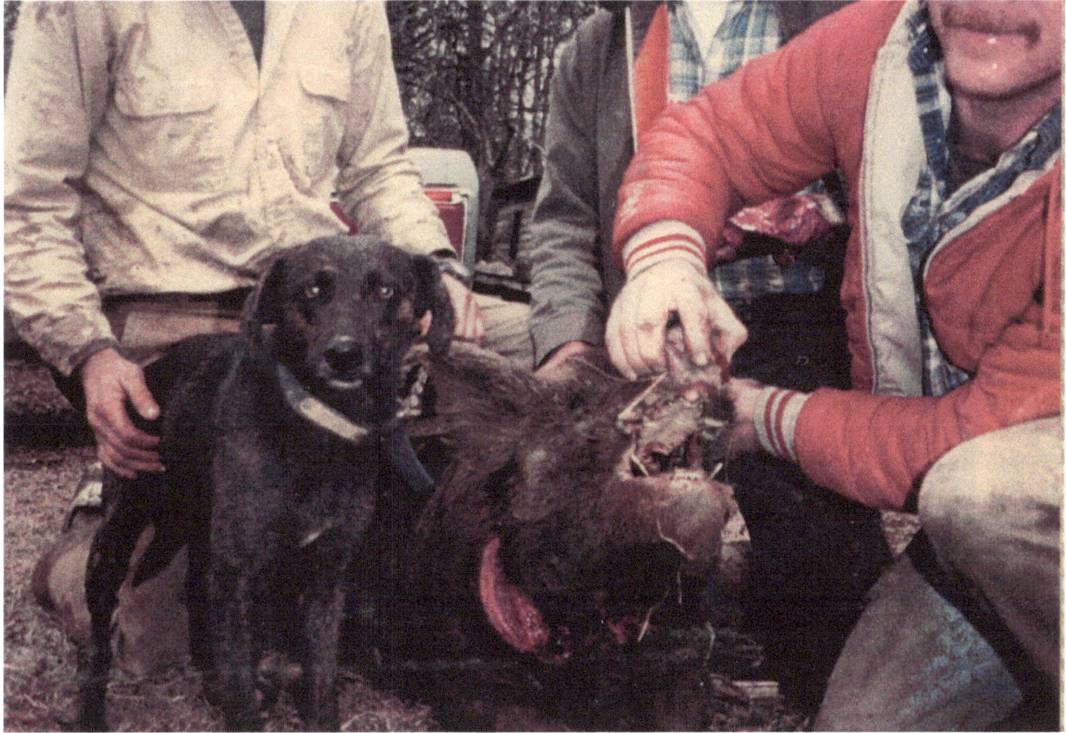

LE on the left beside the Boar that cut Norman Kemmer's hand in Mobile. Larry Biggs is holding the Boar's mouth open, but if you look just under his arm you can see Norman's hand covered with a bloody rag. This day let me know how much a man can bleed and not die.

One of our trips to Mobile saw us spending the night. During a long tough day of hunting we lost LE. Now we had name tags and phone numbers on his collar, so if we lost him we just had to get to a phone and call mama at home and see if anyone had found him. Daddy and them left me at a little camp house that belonged to Larry right on the bank of the river. I would wait with Speck and Slim at camp, Daddy and Carl

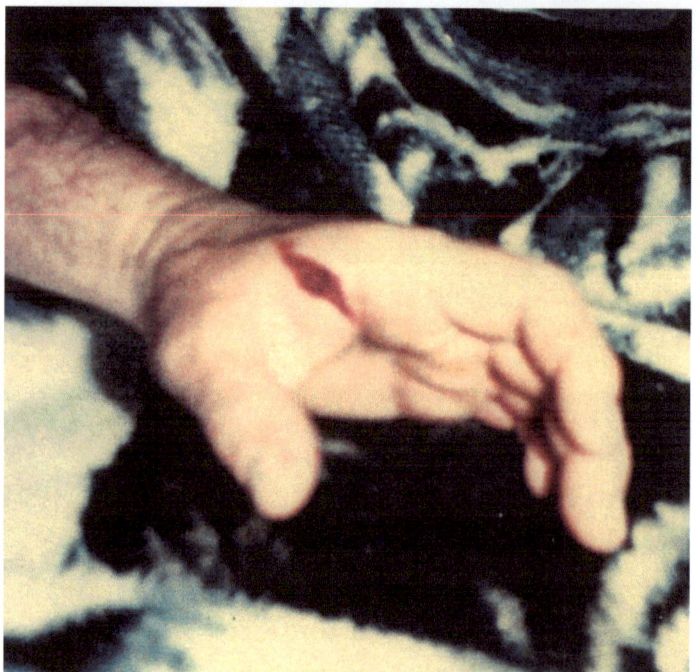

(Above) Larry Biggs in the center with his trusty catch dog Fleas at his side. I could have drug a box spring mattress through the woods and made less noise than this dog made with every step he took. They are standing beside the Boar that cut Daddy's hand.

(Left) Norman Kemmer's hand the day after it was sliced by a boar in Mobile Alabama. He had been cut by another Boar in this exact spot back in the early 70s. The scars made a perfect X after this one healed. You see Scars are tattoo's with a better story.

would take a boat ride to the boat launch under I-10 where it crosses Mobile Bay, call home and hope for good news. I sat on the porch of that little hunting cabin with Speck and Slim both in boxes beside me as the full moon rose on that clear and quiet night. As it got later you could hear every noise in the distance. That area was crawling with Nutria Rats. A small varmint about the size of a small beaver with a rat looking tail. Two of them were just across the river from the camp. I could not only hear them, but I could see the water rippling as they fed. I then began to hear something to my right, also on the opposite side of the river, easing slowly up towards the Nutria. As the sound got close enough I could see a sleek very black figure moving slowly in a stalking crouch. I began to realize that it was a Black Panther. All my life I had heard that they existed but never dreamed I would be lucky enough to actually see one. As he got within striking range of the Nutria he made his move. He pounced and caught the big rat, then turned and began swimming straight across the river in my direction. He did not have a good hold on the Nutria, and it was consistently struggling to get away. I immediately sprang into action. The struggle would keep the Panther's full attention while I removed Speck from his box and slipped to within 15 or so feet of the river's edge. Then I also knew that upon reaching the bank the Panther would then have to stop and readjust hold on the struggling Nutria. I would wait for him to be in the middle of this before my release, and by the time he knew Speck was there it would have been over. I then moved Speck into position while the Panther swam. Everything was going great and we had reached our waiting point. About half way across the river however, the Nutria Rat got away from the Panther's poor hold. After he lost the Rat the Panther turned left and swam out of site from me straight down the river. What a crushing loss. Seeing a Panther is a treat that few enjoy, but had we been able to have snagged him that would have ranked among the coolest of stories.

Oh well, Carl and Daddy returned to the camp, enjoyed the story and informed me that someone had found LE and was going to meet them at the Bay Boat Ramp at daylight with him. They would get him, return to camp, and we would hunt the next day. Now this guy finding LE was a strange event in itself. LE was the kind of dog that my grandfather loved. No one could touch LE except the few people he knew and trusted. But this total stranger said that he was fishing, saw LE on the bank, pulled up and LE jumped in his boat. Now all we could figure was that LE, off after a hog, had had a close encounter with something that scared him, probably a Gator, and wanted to get to safety. Well whatever it was Daddy and Carl left to get him that next morning and told me

This was the Boar that Massacred Slim down under the mud at the end of the day on our first trip to Mobile.

to take Speck and Slim for a short walk down the bank to empty them out, so that when they returned we would be able to get right to the hunt. Well on my short empty out walk me and my crew ran head long into a big group of hogs. I caught four before Daddy and Carl got back with LE. It was a good crew of dogs and that Mobile area provided us with a lot of adventure.

We also began hunting with Carl's cousin just North of there in a town called Jackson Alabama. This was the spot where I saw the highest population of hogs in those days, consequently this was where I saw the highest population of deer as well. On our first trip up there when we arrived Carl's cousin Clark Allday had several guys there planning to hunt with us. He then pointed to this big long lanky six foot six string bean and said I got somebody here to run with Mitch. See when a bunch of men get together they always try to outdo each other. All my life my Daddy beat everyone to the battle site once we broke for it. When catch dogs arrive at a big boar it is only a matter of time before he kills them all, so the goal is to get there as fast as you possibly can, and in his prime no man ever beat my father to a battle site. The first time I outran my father to a hog I was 17 years old. He was leaving his prime and I was entering mine. After that day no man ever beat me to a hog once we all broke for it. Clark had heard Carl say this, plus he had hunted with us at Larry Biggs place. So Clark had collected this long lanky

Charlie Kemmer helping us on a hog killing day. These two Boars were brought out alive from mobile, but it was time to fill the freezer. The Boar he is washing is the one that cut Speck's throat and caused him to almost bleed to death. The one hanging from his feet in the back is the one that cut Slim up so bad on our first trip to Mobile. My Grandfather was the wisest man I ever met. I often referred to him as "The Keeper of the Gates of Wisdom". I loved and respected no man above him.

Alabama track star to run with me. He began listing all the track records this guy had set in high school and college. Daddy and Carl just smiled. Later that day we were in a deep river swamp which was nice and open for the most part, then LE disappeared. As all men and dogs waited on full alert, we heard him bay. Now the rule is to always give the catch dogs a good head start. Daddy usually said when to go. The bay began, Speck bolted ahead, and Daddy gave the go. As I rolled out I passed Slim up, running in those open woods I was airing it out. Suddenly I heard something behind me. I just assumed it was the other catch dogs pouring the coal to it and gaining on me. As I dipped around a tree I glanced back and here came our long tall Alabama racer stretching his long legs out and gaining ground. Unfortunately for him hogs usually bed up, then bay up, in a fine little briar thicket somewhere. So just as his long legs were making up for my initial burst of energy, we hit the thick stuff and it was over. By the time he arrived I had the hog caught and was waiting on him with a nice big smile. All men are not created equal and the hog woods are a constant competition when it is full of Alfa Males. Carl was much like my father, he seldom gave out compliments, but on the day I ran the Palmetto Reed up my nose Carl looked at me and said, "No matter what I do, you always find a way to end the day the muddiest, the bloodiest, and the baddest".

Norman Kemmer to the right and Carl to the left, with our crew of dogs in the Mobile Palmetto Mud Bog Swamp. They are all setting in a huge hog bed, built from hogs collecting and stacking up Palmetto bushes to mound up a bed that would keep them out of the water. Judging by the depth of the mud around it these hogs had built this 20 foot circle bed up about 4 foot in height. A lot of hard work by a lot of smart and determined hogs. This bed was situated in such a way that in the cooler winter months, it caught the first rays of sunlight in the morning. What an amazing accomplishment by such a smart animal.

Our next hunt with Clark found us meeting him at a man's hunting area. The seasons were all closed and the man wanted us to help thin the hog populations out on his deer hunting club. The man also met us there with his sons. They all had rifles, Daddy never allowed anyone to hunt with us and our dogs with guns. Guys tend to get nervous in a tense battle situation and shoot your dogs, or shoot through a hog and hit the dogs. So Daddy laid the law down. They then asked if these catch dogs would be enough. Folks who have never been around real bulldogs do not understand, nor comprehend what they can do. So Daddy launched into this 'Heat Seeking Missile' speech on how a bulldog was better than a gun, but the smirks and sneers on these guys faces let us know they were not buying our superhero talk. The swamp was dry that day and very open. About mid morning we came up on a monster beaver den in an old dried up lake. The entry holes on this den spell out that it was inhabited by a rather large beaver. The dogs were out and about hunting as we walked up on this den. One of those Alabama clucks looked at Daddy and said, "You better hope your bulldogs don't get a hold of one of these beavers. They got giant teeth and will rip a dog to shreds". Daddy kinda chuckled, as Speck came up on our merry little group. Being Speck he went straight into that beaver entrance. I began to hear some rumbling around inside the den so I leaned over to this corn ball and said, "Boy you about to find out how tough them beavers are". I looked up in the den entrance and I could see Speck's butt as he was hunching backwards dragging something out of that hole. I guess quarters were too tight in there and he wanted to get it out in the open for combat. When he drug it out it was around a 50 pound Beaver, by far the biggest I had ever seen. Speck was a 36 pound male and when he got that beaver out clear of that den he went in on it and that dude was Stone Dead in 60 seconds flat. Boy Speck could murder stuff like that. The entire affair drew a big smile from my father.

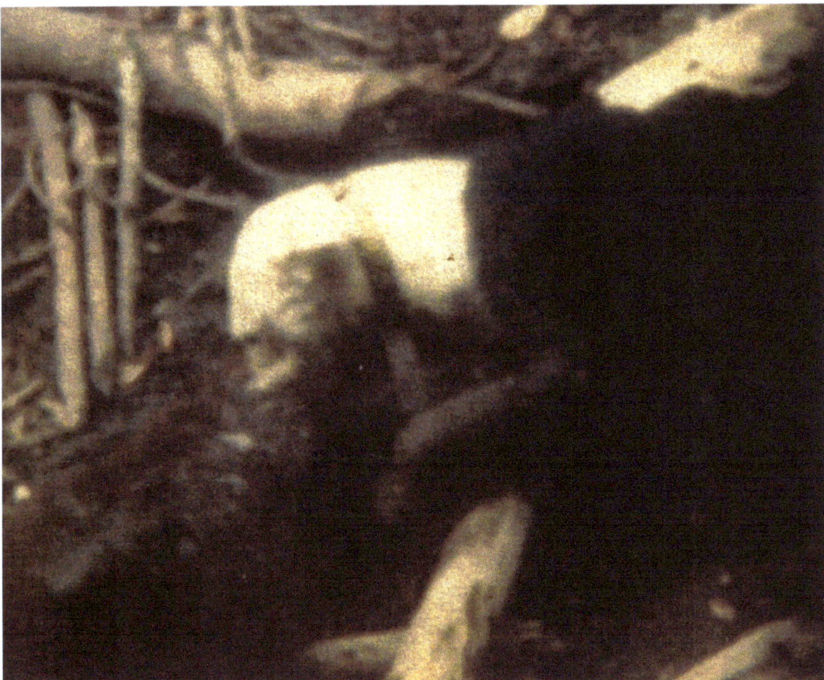

The quality on this photo is poor, but this is Speck killing that huge Beaver in the Alabama Swamps. Speck made short work of his opponent that day, killing him in only seconds. It was beautiful.

Chapter 9
THE ELROD AFFAIR

In the days before GPS systems that one could carry in his pocket, we used a compass in the swamp. Hunting in the Mountains is easy because you go to the top of one, recognize other ones, and get your bearings. In the swamp there is no high point and everything looks the same. In the deep south most rivers run, barring a few twists and turns of course, basically North and South. So if you are hunting the East side of a river, you leave the boat and hunt in East, then when you decide to come back to the river you just head due West. It's not brain surgery. Then when you hit the river your challenge is deciding if you are above or below the boat. Now everyone who hunted with my father always remarked on his incredible ability to hunt all day, zig zag all over the deep swamp and then come straight back to the exact spot on the river where the boat was hidden. I have no idea how he did it, but he did it week after week, even when we hunted in strange places. It was just a great 'sense of direction'.

One of our favorite spots to hunt was on the Pascagoula River. Black Creek angles into the Pascagoula River on it's west side, and this area between the Creek and the River was a fine area for hogs. When you hunted here you were not only in the forks of a creek, but there was a Highway just North of the forks, so basically you were hunting in a triangle. It was a perfect spot to hunt for 'directionally challenged dummies', with no possible way to get lost, at least it would appear that way.

Now I played football, boxed, played baseball, power lifted, and to say the least I did not go through High School unnoticed. I had a lot of friends, and being in the deep South of Mississippi all the guys I knew hunted. So over the years many of them would tag along to the hog woods with me and my father. We hunted every weekend no matter what in this time period, so any buddy who wanted to be around me from 1984 on pretty much would have to go hog hunting. Well hanging out with a rough and rowdy crowd like I did you meet all kinds. I had met a guy named John Elrod, who drove a muscle car and fancied himself a tough enough guy to hang with the group of guys that ran with me. John had some good squirrel hunting woods behind his house that I had taken advantage of on many evenings after school. See I hunted everything, and in the winter every minute that it was day light and I was not involved in school or a sporting event, I was in the woods killing something. John had accompanied me on a few squirrel hunts and then asked to be allowed to go on a hog hunt with us. Well I hesitated because John was a bit of an arrogant acting fellow and the amount of friends that I had hanging around had forced my father to be around enough idiots, that I had gotten to the point of doing him the favor of trying to screen the number of clowns I allowed to hunt with us. But John fancied himself a 'Rambo' type tough guy and I kinda wanted him to get a taste of what he had only experienced setting on his couch watching First Blood. I invited him, and boy did he get his money's worth. Rambo my ass.

They were calling for rain that day, but rain never interrupted a hunt for us, and it was the Pascagoula River / Black Creek triangle that was on the list to hit in our routine for rotating hunting areas. We came in on black creek, boated down it to about a mile before it hit the big River and hit the woods in the triangle. LE bayed and I broke for him, running off and leaving everyone else had became a usual thing for me and I thought nothing about it, but usually Daddy would arrive within a minute or two of my arrival. I always wanted to get there as fast as humanly possible to grab the two back legs of the boar. This threw off his mobility and made him less agile for slicing up dogs. But I arrived at this hog, which was about a 75 pound sow, and no one else arrived. I then put what we called a 'one legging rope' around her back leg, tied her to a tree, and started breaking dogs off. If you leave catch dogs on a small hog like that they will kill her, or at least chew her ears off. By the time Daddy arrived I was done. I looked at him with a strange look on my face and said, "What happened". I could tell he was furious as he spoke. s Daddy was as reliable as the sunrise, and he always got there right after me. He also knew that I was relying on him for help. How much help depended on what size and type of hog the dogs had, which could not be known until arrival. Luckily on this day it was a nothing sow and I did not desperately need help. In his frustrated voice he answered, "I had to wait on that idiot you brought with us". At that point I looked and John was 200 yard away and still poking his ass in our direction. I looked at Daddy and said, "What is wrong with him?". Daddy then told me that when he took off he just decided to look back and make sure that John was on the way, and he could not see him. So he went back to get him within sight, then proceeded to run at a slow enough pace as to keep him in sight so he did not get lost. Now none of this made any sense at all because Daddy was an old man by this point and John was an 18 year old athletic High School kid. This pace John was moving at, you would have thought he was a 400lb fat kid. Well when John arrived on the scene I looked at him and said, "Hey man what's wrong. You've got to keep up". He then snapped at me and said, "Don't worry about me". Now normally when anyone snapped at me I proceeded to whip their ass thoroughly, but as slow as John was moving that morning I figured if I beat him down for his tone, it might slow him even more. Daddy, knowing what I was pondering, then butted in and explained to John how easy it was to get lost in the swamp, how dreadfully important it was that we get to the dogs quickly to help possibly save their lives, and how him keeping up was crucial. John then looked at my father and said, "Don't ever wait for me and don't worry about me. I can take care of myself, I do not need either one of you". Daddy then looked at me and smiled.

About that time LE, who had left as soon as I one legged that sow, bayed about a mile from us. I then bolted in his direction. About half the way to him the bottom fell out of the sky and the hardest down pour of rain began that you can possibly imagine. I could barely hear LE and upon arriving at him there were no catch dogs in site. So I squatted in the bushes and watched as he had a 125 pound red boar bayed up. The rain had obviously thrown off Speck and Slim so I figured they would arrive with Daddy who I knew would be along soon. As I watched a fine bay, I saw Daddy approaching and motioned for him. The catch dogs were not with him. He said he had not seen the catch dogs or John since breaking for the bay bark. We waited and waited, and as the heavy rain continued not catch dogs, nor John arrived. We figured that when the rain began it had hampered Speck and Slims ability to hear LE's bay, then when they doubled back to pick up our trail, they must have found John and stayed with him out of confusion. After about a 30 minute wait we realized that something was wrong so we caught LE and headed for the boat, thinking that John or the catch dogs may work there way back there.

Upon arriving at the boat there was no sign of any of the crew. There was a House Boat parked about 100 feet up the creek from the boat and we got on it to try and wait out the rain. Normally after realizing that we had lost dogs, or in this case a lost person, we would have begun a hollering routine. Nice flat southern river swamp bottoms help sound carry for miles and miles, but the extremely heavy rain that was taking place would have made hearing at even a very short distance impossible. So we waited and waited, but as the day wore on the rain never let up. It went from heavy to very heavy. Now normally the dogs would have worked their way straight back to the boat and the spot that they were released that morning, but by hooking up with a person in our party, they would simply follow him thinking that he knew what he was doing, and boy were they wrong. Knowing they were with him and would not return to the sight, seeing no let up in the rain as it got dark, and knowing John would not move at night, we decided to head home for the night and hoped the rain would stop the next day.

The plan was simple, we would be back in that same spot in the morning as it got daylight, the rain was scheduled to quit about 3 am, and we would find them. Now you have to understand that a person in the swamp can't be found by just walking around looking. Our thought process was that when the rain stopped and it got daylight John would hear the traffic on the Highway North of him, he would also hear boat traffic, including ours, on the River or Creek on each side of him. At that point he could just pick a direction to head to noise and work his way out. Hell he was in a triangle for goodness sake. Had he been lost in the Pearl and walked in the wrong direction, he could have walked for 30 miles and not gotten out. But this triangle he was in, as long as he walked straight in ANY direction for two or three miles, he would be out. We had gotten separated in the very southern tip of the triangle, so hearing boat traffic, with just a short walk would have gotten him to the bank to flag down a boat. Or simply walk into the Sun, or away from the sun. The point is a walk straight in any direction would have put him out of the woods in a matter of a few hours. But most importantly as long as he had a compass, which he was told to be sure and bring, that would have allowed him to continue on a straight path in rain, dark, and without having to hear highway or boat traffic. But after it was all over it seems that John's 'I can take care of myself' attitude had caused him to disregard my instructions to 'be sure and bring a compass'.

As we arrived home that night and told mama of our adventure, and John's continuing adventure, she freaked out. We told her our plans for finding him in the morning when he worked his way out to the River as the rain stopped and the silence in the woods allowed him to hear boat traffic. Well she insisted that we call John's mama and tell her what was going on. Daddy felt that that would only lead to hysteria and panic, and just cause a lot of trouble. He said as soon as the rain stopped John would hear his way out. But mama eventually insisted, and they called John's mama. Then true to Daddy's prediction the hysteria began.

As we arrived at the Pascagoula River boat launch the next morning there must have been a hundred Rescue Squad members on scene. Also John's mama was there with three of John's 'Rambo style' buddies from our High School ready for their dumb helpless asses to hit the swamp in search of poor neglected John. Daddy immediately told those three clucks that if they went into the swamp after John there would be three more clowns that would need found. Daddy then proceeded to explain to the man in charge of the Rescue Squad that now that the rain had stopped that John would hear either Highway Traffic or River Traffic and work his own way out of the triangle he was in. He explained that trying to work a search party into the swamp was useless. About an hour after daylight, as the Rescue Squad man ignored Daddy's advice and was organizing for a 'spread out swamp search' John made his way to the river bank, having heard the boat traffic, and flagged down a passing boat. Imagine that. Within thirty minutes of the pick up John was at the Rescue Squad bus with us and his panic stricken mother and 3 Rambo friends who all had their 18 inch knives strapped to their hips.

When he arrived at the bus he only had Speck with him. After giving him ample time to play the hero that he was being treated as, instead of a dumb ass teenager who can't keep up with an old man, I approached him to ask about Slim. When I did he launched into this long hero story about his 'unbelievable adventure' of the last 18 hours. Now my experience with lost dogs, especially in heavy rain, is that when they realize they are lost, and you are lost (because they can tell), they usually just fall in behind you and walk. Again this is especially true in a hard down pour. But John's was a wild adventurous story of hunting and catching hogs all the way to the water's edge that morning. According to John's story they caught a total of four hogs, the last of which was a monster boar that killed Slim. Now keep in mind this is someone who has never been on a hog hunt in his life. His mother and three Rambo friends were not only engrossed in the story but kept congratulating him on his heroism. I asked how did you get the dogs off these hogs, because we break them off with a breaker stick which John did not have. A breaker stick is used to pry the mouth open. John's reply was that he simply pulled them off. I then walked back to Daddy and explained to him that I had closely inspected Speck before putting him in the box and he did not have even a small scratch on him. Daddy said to me quietly, "Well we know the little shit is lying, but we do need to know about Slim, so that we know whether or not to keep looking for him." What Daddy and I strongly suspected was that he had simply left Slim in the woods. See Slim hated crossing water and in those river swamps crossing slues was a common thing. Slim hated crossing and would hesitate to do so. Speck would bolt right into water and loved to swim, but Slim would wait at the water's edge hoping that someone would help him across. We never did and simply walked off and he would eventually cross and catch up. But we suspected that John may have helped him the first time or two, got Slim to expecting and waiting for the help, then John simply got tired of helping and left him. So to find out John's final reply on Slim I pushed my way through his hero worship group for one last question session. I said, "Look John, I need to know the truth on Slim, because if he is not actually dead then Daddy and I need to go look for him". Then I asked if he was sure if Slim was dead and he looked at me and took his finger and slide it across his throat and said, "His throat was cut from ear to ear and he is dead". He added, "I was lucky to get Speck off and save him". His mother then sighed in a relieved manner that even John had survived. I then looked at John again and said, "Your are sure he is dead.....Stone Dead". John looked at me and said, "Yes, he is Stone Dead". As the words 'stone dead' rolled off of John's tongue a voice came over the radio in the front of the Rescue Bus and said, "We just found the other dog". With that, my eyes still looking into John's eyes, I shook my head and walked back to Daddy. We then went to the river's edge to wait for the boat that was carrying Slim. As he arrived he also did not have a mark on him, confirming what Daddy and I had suspected about John's wild adventure stories.

John and I never hung out after that. As he returned to the usual hang out areas of that day, I think he thought that everyone would hail him the hero that his mother, the rescue squad, and his 3 Rambo friends did on that day. That was not the case. For years after the 'Elrod Affair' any real guys that saw him anywhere would ask him if he needed help getting home that night. If he mentioned leaving an area to go to somewhere else, someone would ask if he was sure he knew how to get there. But the most common was every time he would drive off many would holler "Don't get lost now". Well so much for John.

Chapter 10
Speck and Slim

We rolled on with Speck, Slim, and LE, then added for a while a new member to the group. My family has had a very long history in dogs. The Kemmer's got to Tennessee in 1806 and there was another family called the Fords who were already there. The Ford's had two cur dogs and crossed them giving the Kemmer's a few pups. Then my family proceeded to keep that same line of dogs since that day. They are now known as the Kemmer Stock Curs, and are popular nation wide for hunting squirrels, coon, mountain lions, and of course hogs. It was a Kemmer Cur that we added to our crew that we had gotten from our cousin Robert Kemmer. His name was Trapper. He was a high geared dog and as we would proceed through the woods on a hunt he would proceed to cover every square inch of ground within 500 yards of every single step we took. We would, over the years, hunt a number of Kemmer Dogs and have very good success with them. With our crew we would roll on catching hogs from the Sabine River on the Texas / Louisiana border to South Florida. During this time period we did our best to hunt at least once a week. Daddy was dogging in other dog sports as well and that kept him, and eventually me as well, busy on weekdays with conditioning, and on many Saturdays with that sport as well, but we did our best to squeeze in a hog hunt at least once a week. That may be a Saturday or a Sunday, or a day we would get rained out of work on a brick job. During this time frame we were catching around 70 to 80 hogs a year. This was about 40 to 60 hogs a year more than any of the other hog hunters that we were associated with during that same time frame. This proved what a fine working dog crew we had, and also that Daddy's 'playing for the fast break' style of hunting was the best by far to score on the thin populations of heavily hunted hogs in the day.

On this day Norman, Mitch, and Jack Kemmer were hunting the Pearl River. This is a sow we caught in the edge of a slue on that day. Speck is on one ear at the left, Trapper on the other ear, Slim behind Trapper caught on a front leg, and then there is trusty little LE making his usual assist on the butt area. LE believed in 'safety first'.

We were hunting the Cat Island straight out in the Gulf a few miles from Long Beach Mississippi. Who ever owned that Island had stocked it with pure Russian hogs. Other than it being a dry salt sea air miserable place to be, the action out there was fun. The Island had Fallow Deer on it, all the squirrels were fox squirrels, the hogs were nice beautiful Russians, the Gators were thick, and it proved a lot of action. One day we were out there and ran across something that looked like a Wolverine, but we never lucked up and got a bulldog attached to one so we didn't get a picture. Once we were out there and came up on some sort of Satanic Worship Site. It was all a cool experience.

We had also been hitting an old site of Daddy's which was the NASA Test site where him and Dave caught the Rhinoceros Boar. Now NASA security was always there, but

Norman Kemmer driving the boat home after a good day of hog hunting. That is Cat Island in the background. Notice the little 'scifk type' boats that we hunted with. We had 20 HP motors on the backs.

it had tightened a great deal, and of course no hunting was allowed. Now again we are in a grey area because a hog is not a game animal, plus we do not have guns, etc., but our policy had become to not allow anyone to catch us so we could just avoid the conversation at all. We had even gotten out of the days of Daddy and Wayne picking on Game Wardens. We had long been hiding the boat,

A nice Russian Sow one legged to a tree on Cat Island. Notice the good European Bloodline that had been put on this privately owned Island.

Cat Island in the mid 80s. This was the Satanic Area we found on the Island. During this time frame, Waco Texas among other areas were having outbreaks of Satanic Cults and silly stuff like that, so we found this quite entertaining.

covering tracks, and just avoiding contact with the law all together. So our entrance into NASA was no different. We had a spot we could drive in to within about 2 miles of the check in gate on the test site. We would arrive there way before day light, walk in, and be in the test sight area long before the sun rose. Once we were in open woods a good Navy Seal team would have had trouble finding us. Problems usually occurred at the boat or vehicle on the load out, so we just ran a dummy run out a mile or two empty, then came back for the real pick up.

On this day in NASA, after a hard days hunt we caught a nice little 125 pound black boar. As we got back to the road where the NASA Guard shack entrance was, it was about 4 pm and we still had about 3 hours until dark. It had been a long hard hunt and we were both tired having left the house at 2 am to get in before light. Now that entrance road into the check in gate is flat as it could possible be and you can see down it for miles. So Daddy scouted for a crossing as I waited with our catch and the dogs. Upon his return he laid out the choices for me. We could wait until dark, go down the road about 2 miles to get out of site of the guard shack, or we just cross and let them see us. Being the adventurer that I had always been, I said, "Let's cross here and let those guards have some fun trying to catch us". Daddy agreed, then explained that he would cross with the dogs first and get them under the fence on the far side. Then after he had crossed the fence I could start. Now that meant that his crossing would alert the guards, so it would be my crossing that would be the risky one. As he explained that to me I laughed and said, "Let's get it". He went across and true to form the guards poured out of that shack and to their vehicles. As I crossed the road with a live tied hog on my shoulders, I looked towards the shack and the truck was on it's way. I reached the fence on the other side and slid the hog under the fence. After crossing I pick him up again and heard the truck stop and the door open. They were within 15 feet of me and I was carrying a hog. After rolling about 10 feet I could hear them pinging the barbed wire as they crossed the fence behind me. 30 more feet and I was expecting hands to be grabbing me and it would be time to drop the hog and begin their ass whippings, but there was nothing. I ran about 100 yards and got curious, so I stopped and looked back, hog still on my shoulders. They both had jumped the fence, but had stopped after about 10 feet and were standing there looking at me. Disappointed with their lack of effort, I put one arm up in the air and waved for them, and at the same time holler, "Come on Boys". Daddy, about 50 yards in front of me yelled to me, "Shut up boy and come on". So I turned and went to him. Damn lazy ass guards, this story could have been so much better had they had any kind of a sack between them.

Proof of what a fine working crew we had in LE, Speck, and Slim came one morning when we got a call from a guy in Pishtosh Town Mississippi. Now Pishtosh Town was full of folks with the last name of Ladner. When my grandfather was teaching me to drive he told me that when you go to pull onto a road, I was to look both ways, pull out, and expect to be hit immediately by a Ladner. So one day when driving through Pishtosh Town, or Ladnerville, on our way to Diamond Head for a hunt, There was a Ladner pulled off the road in the grass talking to another Ladner. As Daddy went to drive by, all of a sudden with no signal, nor warning, the trusty Ladner did an absolute 90 degree bolt across the road with his vehicle. Any by stander that saw how he waited until the very last second to bolt across would have insisted that this idiot was committing suicide. Well Daddy was forced to T-Bone him right in the side of his truck. As we all got out of our vehicles, he stepped back over to his and flipped his blinker on, then killed his engine. He had devised a plan that when the cops arrived to take the accident report, he would show them that his blinker, which of course he had not used during the incident, was on. This would make him look in the right. Daddy, having seen what he had done, told Dave Mitchell who was in for the weekend and hunting with us, that while Daddy got the two Ladner's attention, that Dave was to slip over to the man's vehicle and switch that blinker back off. So Dave did just that. When the cops arrived for the report the lying Ladner proceeded to play the innocent victim and explain that he had put his blinker on, then easily and slowly crossed the road. Then he insisted to the officer that he could prove it, and walked to his truck to turn on the ignition. As he did, he backed up to look, and guess what, no blinker. Until this day I know that conniving Ladner is still bumfuzzled over his foiled lie. But back to our well oiled crew.

We got a Pishtosh town call one day with talk of this ghost hog that was destroying corn field after corn field and no one could catch it. The man explained how every local hog hunter in the area had been trying to catch this hog for almost a year. The man said he had given up and called us. We arrived that morning and were being driven in to where the hog sign was. Growing up hunting everything with my Grandfather, I had my head hanging out the window on the drive in looking for tracks on the road. All of a sudden I yelled, "Stop the truck". As they stopped I got out to investigate. I walked back up to the truck and explained that not only had I found a fresh track, but that it was about 60 seconds old. The mud was still falling back in the fresh track. We dropped LE out first, then Speck and Slim right behind him. In about 80 yards LE barked once and the Cavalry arrived. It was a monster sow and I arrived a few seconds behind Speck and Slim. When it was all over the man proceeded to shake his head in amazement. He said that everyone within 50 miles of him had been after this hog, some running her for as much as 10 hours in one day. He said that he looked at his watch when LE hit the ground and we had her caught with me attached to her leg in 90 seconds. See if we had just turned LE loose we would have had a race. If we had led our bulldogs up, she would have broke and we would have had a race. Playing for the 'fast break' and this ghost hog was caught in 90 seconds.

This Ghost Sow had a big wart looking thing on her neck. When we skinned her out, she had a 30 Caliber bullet lodged in her neck. We killed hogs all the time that had lead in them. Hogs are not like deer, they can take some lead. We caught a big sow in a huge briar patch in Beaumont Mississippi one time. That briar patch was a hot spot for rabbit and even deer hunters. When we ate this Beaumont Sow we found so much lead that we kept a small cup on the table and we would drop any lead we found

The Pishtosh Town Sow we caught in 90 seconds. This sow had given all the local hog hunters in our area the run a round, then they called us in. Notice the 'wart like' spot on her neck. We found a 30 caliber rifle bullet lodged in her neck. 90 seconds after dropping the tailgate and she was toast.

in her, into that bowl. We found everything from birdshot to buckshot, and we also found 3 30 caliber pieces of lead in her. No telling how many times she had been shot, but nothing a good catch dog can't stop.

In the hog hunting world when a hunter hunts a certain area enough he tends to believe that that is his hunting area, and no one else should be there. We often had run ins with this sort of thing. In the old days Daddy hunted a bit with a neighbor of ours named Phillip Holland. Phillip never quit hunting during the slow years that Daddy and Jack turned their attention to other dog sporting events, but since our return to the hog woods Phillip had become more of a competitor hog hunter than someone we hunted with. Unlike us Phillip only hunted locally, and had teamed up with another local hog hunter named Mitch Moran. Mitch's cousin Timmy Moran worked with us so we kept up with what their success rate was through Timmy, and they did the same, again through Timmy as well. With the Speck, Slim, and LE crew we were averaging at least 80 hogs a year. This Holland / Moran crew were lucky to average 12 to 15 a year. We found the comparison comical, and they did not.

I was 19 years old and to say I was 'full of fire' would have been a bold understatement. I have had many chapters in my life, but in this time frame I had a street fighting chapter mingled in with my hog hunting and my other dog sport chapters. I was very hot headed to say the least. One night me and a friend, Travis Northrup, were in a local store where we lived and Phillip walked up to me. Now Phillip is around 50 years old at this time. He began to tell me that he had heard that me and Daddy had been stealing his hogs that he had released in Diamond Head Mississippi. Yes the same Diamond Head / Pine Hills area that Daddy and Jack had been hunting since the late 60s. The worst part of this was the tone in which he was talking to me in. See no one, other than my father, was allowed to speak to me with anything resembling a tone, not ever. As the talk began, Travis walked up behind me and grabbed my shoulders, and whispered in my ear, "He's an old man". As Travis helped me from the store all wild eyed, I went straight home. Travis teased me all the way home as my head was exploding. As I relayed the story to my father, his reaction was the same. See I was a hot head, but my temper could never hold a candle to my father's.

That very weekend we made a point of hunting Diamond Head. We had no thought of running into these clowns in the woods, but did intend to hunt there for several weeks and make a huge dent in the population of hogs there to satisfy our anger. Now when hunting in the woods it is very rare to run into another group of hunters, but low and behold that very day we walked head long into Phillip Holland and Mitch Moran. As soon as Daddy saw them he took off the little hunting pack he had on and handed it to me. I knew exactly what this meant .... and so did Phillip when he saw the pack being handed off. At this point you need to know that my father lived and died without ever meeting the man who could take him in combat. He also lived that life meeting only a few who were willing to try. Daddy had a look about him that spelled 'danger', and I often remarked to my tough street fighting friends that any man who saw Daddy and proceeded to mess with him, deserved what they got. Well on this day in the woods Phillip Holland, nor Mitch Moran, were dumb enough to ignore that look my father had. Now I was surprised that Daddy even spoke, I expected that he would just commence to beating Phillips skull in. Phillip himself also seemed to feel the same way. I saw the relief in his eyes as Daddy started cussing. Phillip and Mitch immediately dropped their heads and began staring at their shoes. Once the shaming and cowering were done, and it was evident that the two Beta Males had been put in there place, the hunt continued. Now we had walked head long into them, which meant that we were going where they had been, and they were going where we had been. All of a sudden we looked ahead and Slim was rolling in something. He had found a pile of human shit and was rolling in it. Dogs can never pass a pile of human shit without hitting it for a roll. Daddy was furious. As we approached the truck, Slim still covered from head to toe in feces, Daddy began cussing again. See Slim was Daddy's dog and we each loaded our own dogs. Daddy

(Top) Mitch Kemmer in the center, with Trapper on the left, and Slim lying down on the right. (Middle) My mother, Carolyn Kemmer, holding a baby wild pig in one photo. In the other, (bottom)she has Speck on the left and LE on the right.

looked at me and said in a loud disgusted voice, "I've got to load this damn dog, and him covered in PHILLIP HOLLAND SHIT". I never laughed at my father, except on this day, it was impossible not to. You see to say that Phillip Holland was not a very hygienic man, would be putting it mildly. To understand his bathing and teeth brushing habits makes the entire affair more comical. I still enjoy a laugh every time I think of that day.

We awoke on September 19, 1987 and headed for trusty Bogalusa. We were going to hunt the forks of two slues where Death seemed to haunt us. Bonnie, Mo, Matilda, Itch, Scratch, and many other good bulldogs had died in this area we called 'the forks'. Now most normal people reading this might ask, why would you go to a place to hunt where you had had so much bad luck. Those of you geared like me and my father need not ask, but the forks was our destination. Bad boars had a tendency to reside there and that's the kind we liked. Sows and pigs were fun because you got to see the dogs work, but the real juice was catching the bad ones. One of my best friends named Brian Cumberland would accompany us to the woods on this day. This was not his first hog hunt with us, but it would be his last.

Many times on a hunt, we would take a 10 minute break about 2 pm in the afternoon. This one such break sees Norman Kemmer in the middle lying down. Speck in the front and Slim lying just on the other side of Daddy's feet. This was one hell of a crew. This is also my favorite photo ever taken of Speck.

We hit the woods and had a very nice day. It was hot and the mosquitoes were out in force. After hours into a good hard hunt with a lot of walking we were traveling down the bed of an old slue. Speck and Slim were right with me, and Daddy and Brian were to my left scouting for sign. LE then drifted out to my right, nose in the air, and bayed about 120 yards from me. The swamp was clear where we were and I could see LE standing there baying, then I saw a red boar stand up, shake off and stretch, and face the oncoming attack of Speck and Slim. It was text book and I could see it all. They were approaching him wide open running about 15 feet apart. Just as they reached him he went from a dead stand still, to bolting right between them. He ran straight towards me and came within 10 feet of me. I could have kicked him, but the rule is to be perfectly still until a bulldog is attached to him. So I stood as Speck, Slim, and LE all came rolling by me right on his butt. They were rolling and LE was making a little squeaking bark a little along while the sight race was going. We could hear him for about a half a mile, then everything went to total silence. This could only mean that they had him caught and LE was caught as well. We ran as far as we could in the direction we were sure of, but then it was a situation where you had to stop and just listen. Meandering here and there could easily get you way off the mark. As we waited and listened it was pure torture for me and Daddy because we knew they were caught, since the hog itself was silent we knew it had to be a tough boar, which meant that Speck and Slim desperately needed our help. It was a helpless feeling. As we waited and the mosquitoes began to attack us, Brian began slapping at the aggravating insects. Daddy being frustrated and trying to listen for the slightest sound freaked completely out. Now when I saw my father aggravated I knew that everyone in his presence had better walk light on all toes, so I just allowed the mosquitos to feast on me, but Brian was not so smart. Daddy launched into the necessity of silence needed at this point and how the dogs lives could depend on it. Oddly enough he was doing this at the top of his lungs. But I knew it was him venting his frustration over the situation.

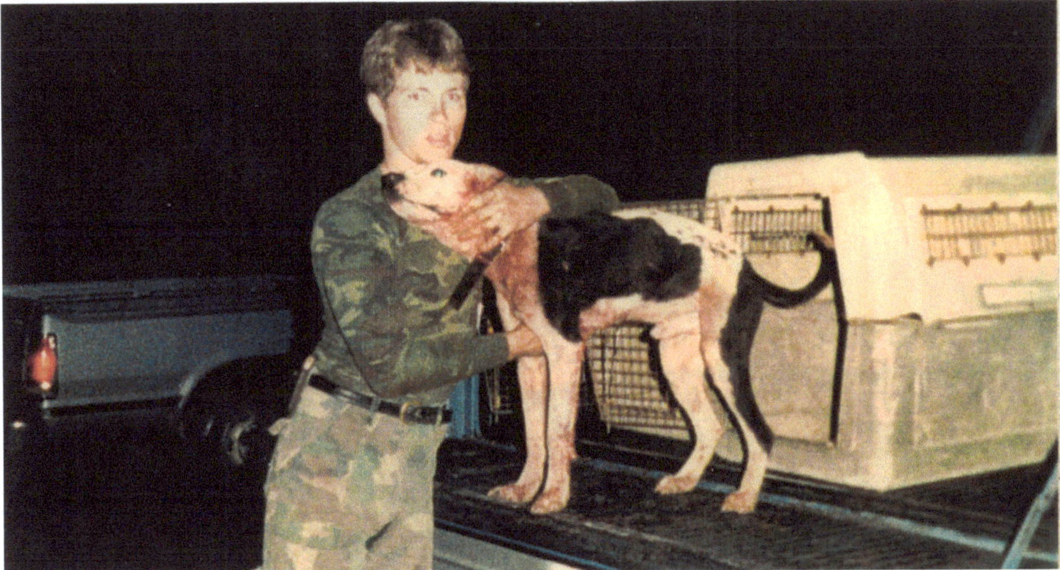

Mitch Kemmer unloading his bloody little Speck dog after a night hunt. I released Speck on this Boar from about 15 yards out, and bolted in right behind him. Even with arriving in seconds this Boar cut Speck 9 times from his head to his tail. One stick was in his jaw, one straight in at the base of his tail, and the other 7 were dispersed everywhere in between. What a fine Boar and what a fine catch dog.

After about 40 minutes of us having to deal with the situation at hand we heard a bark. The first one we could not get a good direction on, but were on full alert when the second came about 5 minutes later. This bark every 5 or 10 minutes that proceeded could only mean one thing. The Boar was free enough to cause LE to worry enough to turn loose, back off, and bark. Each bark, however far between them, got us a little closer. When I got two in a row at one point and zeroed in I blew forward like a freight train. I ran as far as I could without needing another bark to direct me, then I stopped. I then heard a strange sound, and listening for any hint of a noise I ran quickly towards it. The sound I was hearing was extremely heavy breathing from several exhausted animals. Arriving at the battle site, the aftermath of Pickett's Charge could not have impressed me more. They had caught him in a big green briar thicket. They had beaten down a circle about 20 yards across, Speck lay dead in the very center of it, and Slim, LE, and the Boar were laying just at the edge of it, and blood was everywhere. The trio were all laying exhausted on their sides right next to each other. Slim had the Boar caught, but none of them could stand. Even as I grabbed the Boars back leg, he never even flinched. We got the dogs chained to a tree, the Boar tied, and sat for a minute to allow them to rest. As we sat there, my father looked at me and said, "We've lost a Comrade". Speck had been cut 24 times. The ones that killed him hit the main arteries in his neck. Slim was cut 14 times, mostly in the back hind quarter. Of course the barking from LE would have began after Speck fell off dead. What a fine day. What a fine Battle. What a fine Death. Better to die now covered in blood, than like ole Hombre suffering from old age and eventually lying in his own piss. What a lucky dog Speck was, and what a lucky man I was to have owned him.

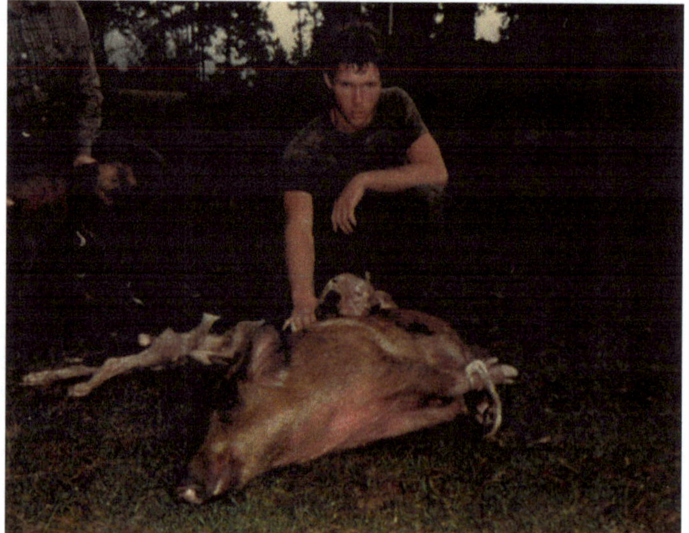

These are photos to the right are of one of the saddest days of my life. This is the day we lost Speck. The Boar that killed him was not a big boar, nor did he have very large teeth, what he did have was the time to kill. If you cannot get to your dogs to help them quickly, death is always the result.

(Below right) Mitch Kemmer holding Speck at the battle sight in the Forks of Bogalusa. Several neck shots hit arteries. Death in Battle is what each true Warrior prays for all his life, but this death came too soon for me.

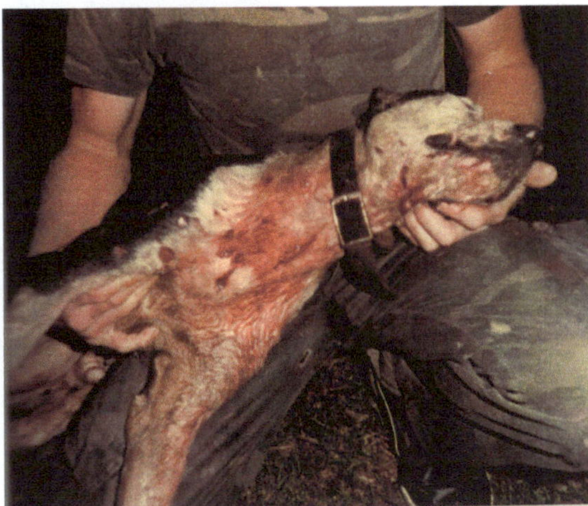

On September 29th, 10 days later, we hit the very same Bogalusa Forks on another trip. We had seen a monster track the day we lost Speck, but the hog we caught was not him. So back we went for this boar. We had LE and only Slim as a catch dog. Jack was living in Tennessee at this point and had a full brother to Slim he was going to bring us, but he had not yet arrived. We got into some good sign and the tracks were the one we had came to find. Off and alone both times we had found his sign, we felt certain it was a big Boar off by himself. We were right. LE bayed and off we all broke. We traveled through some thick stuff, but as I arrived LE continued to bay. Daddy then arrived and the baying continued. We then assumed that Slim had gotten tangled in the thick stuff and would arrive soon. I had often outran Slim to a battle sight. We waited long enough and figured something had to be bad wrong. LE had the Boar bayed in a thicket just in front of us, so we eased in slowly, as not to spook him, for a closer look. When we got where we could see him Slim lay dead at his feet. The Boar had caught him coming in with one good shot straight into his left sink hole in his chest. It stabbed into his heart and he was surely gone in seconds. It had all happened so fast that LE never even missed a bark.

We had lost them both 10 days apart. My father, and later myself, owned better dogs than either of them were, but they made quite a team. Most importantly for me it was that they were with me through the height of my interest in dog hunting for hogs. I do not know if it was their loss, and my disappointment with future dogs we would hunt, but I would soon join my father and my uncle Jack in the other dog sport. We would never stop hog hunting ever again, but my heart for it seemed to die along with Speck and Slim in the Bogalusa Forks, where we had lost many fine Warriors. This book will continue just as we did, because I understand that the best thing you can do with death is ride off from it, but Speck and Slim would be my 'High Water Mark' in my lifetime of Hog Hunting. I loved them both as much as I am capable of loving anything.

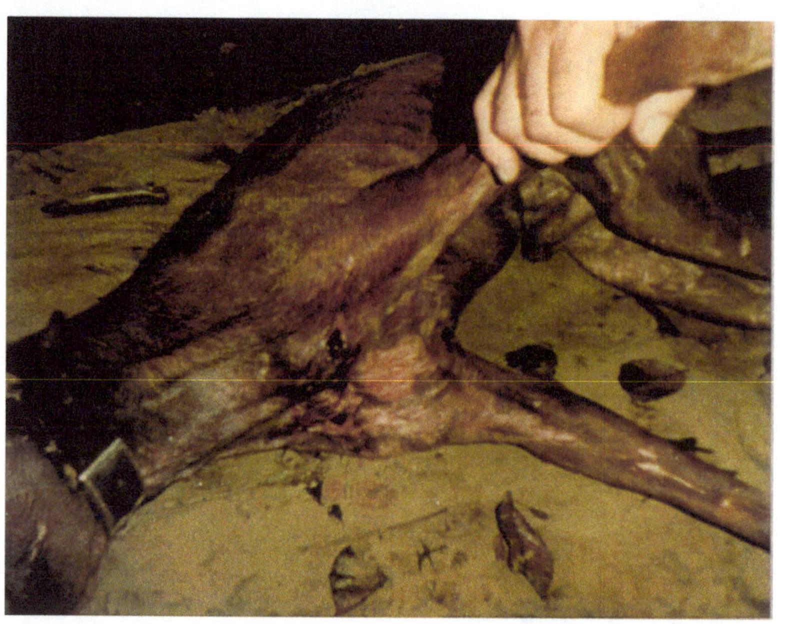

Slim's answer to his prayer came 10 days after the death of Speck. One straight in shot to the sink hole in his chest. This punctures the heart, and death occurs within 15 to 20 seconds. Slim died with hog hair from his opponent in his mouth. What a fine boy. We took him home to sacred ground and buried him with his partner Speck. The dirt from digging Speck's grave was still soft. It was a sad time.

Now telling old school hunting stories in years to come many hog hunters commented on the fact that had we had Kevlar Vests in the old days it would have prevented the number of deaths that we had among catch dogs, so let's spend a minute on cut vests. First I wish I had been the man who came up with the idea of promoting them to hog hunters because by gosh they have bought in. So let's start with the basics. When you join the military or a police force where Kevlar Vests are used, the first thing they tell you is not to be under the mistaken assumption that you are invincible because while that vest will protect you from a bullet, an old woman could come up to you and stab a knife right through that Vest. It is a threaded material and will catch, and stop, a bulky item like a chunk of lead, but anything that starts with a fine point will slide right in. Well that means that if that Boar decides to shoot you with, lets say the handgun he is carrying, then you are safe. But those shank style knives he has sticking out of the side of his face, will blow right through that kevlar with just the strength of an old woman behind it. If someone does not believe this then take your kevlar vest, lay it on the ground, and smoothly stick your knife right through it. kevlar will stop a slash, but not a straight in stick with a tush. So here is the thing to know about kevlar and where it is needed. No slash to the body will kill a dog. A hard blow to the side, may snap that rib and puncture a lung, but kevlar won't stop that. The only thing other than broken ribs that will kill a dog to the body is a straight in 'sink hole shot' in the chest. A slash to the chest will not go deep enough to get the heart, and means nothing. Only that straight in shot kills to the body and with your knife test, you will know that kevlar will not stop that straight shot. So a Kevlar Vest to cover the body is WORTHLESS. It only protects against a few slashes and scrapes, which will not kill him and what that kevlar Vest covering the body is famous for doing is causing him to over heat and die. Yes Kevlar Body Vests kill more dogs from a heat stroke than anything else it achieves. Dog men know this so a lot of them carry the vest with them, lead the bulldog to the battle site, then put the vest on within site of the hog, then release. But if that hog breaks as the catch dog approaches then unless he is a big enough cur to stop when he gets hot, he will join the chase until he dies of a heat stroke. Also if you are hunting in a place where you have the time to lead a catch dog up that close to a bay, your hogs must not have been hunted much. That would never work on the 'Playing for the Fast Breaks' style of hunting that we did. Hogs won't stand there for that. If they hold bay enough for you to lead that close, vest up, then release, and him still stand for all of that, then hell just go up and build a pen around him while he stands, and leave the catch dog out of the equation all together. No hog would be caught in Ansley Mississippi like that. No, that Kevlar Body Vest is worthless for keeping a Boar from killing your dog, and death waiting to happen in a heat stroke.

Many years in the future I will run a Hog Hunting Lodge, and I had a guy by the name of Mitch Spaulding come up from Florida to hunt with me. He, his wife, and his son came to the lodge to catch a Pure Russian, which they did not have in Florida, with their catch dog. He was a white male they had owned since he was 5 weeks old. They asked me to put them on the baddest Russian we could find. They wanted one to put on the wall with the many Desoto Ferals that this dog had caught. Now these were real true dog hunting hog hunters. They began showing me their new kevlar vest that they had for this hunt. They then asked what kind of kevlar vests I used on my dogs. This led me to launch into the kevlar talk I have given in the above paragraph. Mitch then proceeded to tell me that this vest had some new material in it, in addition to the kevlar, and nothing could penetrate it. I then said, "It's material isn't it", and I told him to try and stick his knife through it. He laughed as if I were an idiot who just wasn't up on the new technology. I then said, "Well it's your dog". As the hunt began the next morning we were easing through the woods and began to hear a Boar fight in progress. As we slipped up it was about a 350 pound pure Russian in combat with about a 700 pound Feral Boar. As we got within sight of them we knew we had to let them see us. hopefully they would then separate and run and we could single out the Russian. Well it worked, but as they separated and moved apart, I noticed about 50 holes in the big Feral's side. Not worthless slashes that mean nothing, but straight in 'stick holes'. This clued me in quickly that not only was the Russian tough enough to take on a Boar twice his size, but the straight in shots told me he was a pure athlete, and very talented. As the Russian left slowly he was doing it in a quartering away style as to keep his eye on us, and posturing in such a way as to let us know that he was not scared of us. Mitch and his crew began vesting up their catch dog quickly, as leading him around with the vest on would have already killed him, which they knew from experience. Once vested they released. The Boar keeping his eye on us, saw the oncoming dog, got set for him, dipped down and put his shoulder and half his body into the blow, hit their dog right in the chest. I was filming and told the gentleman to my right, "He just killed that Dog". The guy said, "No way". I said, "He'll be dead in 15 seconds". Being seasoned hog hunters Mitch and his crew quickly grabbed a back leg as their male drifted off into the afterlife. The hog was caught and they had a brief second to say goodbye to there catch dog, bleeding out with that nice new kevlar technology wrapped around him. The Boar had hit one of the sink holes, stabbed the heart and the tears from the Spaulding family rightfully came forth. After removing the vest, I picked it up and filmed it as I stuck my finger through the nice hole that Boar had put through it. If that Boar had only used a pistol, that fine catch dog would still be alive.

Now there is one spot on a dog that a slashing type cut can kill him, and that is his throat. So a good wide Kevlar Collar makes all the sense in the world. Those main arteries that run under that dogs throat can be opened up with the slightest razor cut, and a cut collar will stop that. That means that kevlar can serve a purpose, just not as a body cover, or a vest. A kevlar Cut Collar could have saved Speck for example, because the lethal cuts that killed him were throat slashes. But a Kevlar Cut Vest would not have saved Slim because his was a straight in 'sink hole' shot that hit his heart. Plus if Speck and Slim had had on Kevlar Cut Vests on the day that Speck got killed they would have both died of a heat stroke in the chase and the hog would have gotten away.

This is also a good place to mention another common screw up by most hog hunters, and that is Stapling a dogs wounds. Any sensible doctor will tell you to never, under any circumstances, sew up an animal bite. Bites are basically poison with all the bacteria in a mouth and on teeth. Because of this an animal wound needs to be left open to drain as it heals. Therefore on 95% of all hog slashes, they need to be left completely alone. Our rule always was that, "If the dog can get to it and lick it, it will be fine". Now we had some that got cut on their heads and the tops of there backs, where they could not lick it, so we kept those places full of vaseline, or an antibiotic type salve to keep it open. This heals from the inside out, closes up nicely, and usually does not even leave a scar. Now stapling is bad because it closes the cut up, but if stapled loosely it will work. But my experience is that hog hunters tend to like to brag about the number of staples a dog took after a rough hog, which leads to their tendency to over staple to give them more bragging rights. Closing the wound causes the worst of infections, because it keeps the poison in, which delays the healing to say the least, and makes it have to bust and drain over this delaying process, and makes for a terrible scar. I have seen closed wounds heal slowly, then months later have to bust and drain again, causing more down time for the animal, and on occasion I have seen a wound take a year to eventually heal. Trapping all the infection on the inside is the result of Stapling. We never put a stitch or a staple in a dog.

One time we caught a bad boar with a bulldog female that my Pa had called Sabrina. As I approached the battle site, I began to see a string of guts stretched out for the last 30 feet into the Boar. He had cut her hide at her stomach and her guts fell out and caught on a limb. The Boar had drug her that 30 feet before we arrived. We caught the

Boar, broke her off, and walked back that 30 feet picking up her guts and holding them in our arms. We then got her away from the action and crammed the guts back into her stomach. We than took a roll of duct tape and taped around her waist to hold them in as she healed. Amazingly enough they were all in tact and none were torn, just a 30 foot trail of small intestine. We kept the tape on for about 2 weeks, then removed it and she was fine. The best part is that she hunted the following Saturday and caught another hog, duct tape and all.

Norman Kemmer to the right and Mitch Kemmer to the left. This is a sow we caught deep in the Swamp on Christmas Eve night. It is one of my favorite photos of me and my father. My Grandmother, Agnes Kemmer, was very old fashioned. The kind of old fashioned woman that could make a marriage work from the time it takes place until death. She could do this through the long lost female art of putting the men in the family first. At Sunday dinner at her house the other women, nor the children, were allowed to fix their plates until the men had their plates, which of course were supposed to be fixed by their wives. Well all my life we opened Christmas Presents at my Grandparent's house on Christmas Eve. Well on this Christmas Eve me and Daddy caught this hog deep in the Swamp and did not get home until 11:30 pm that night. I was 17 at this point, and was considered a man in my Grandmother's eyes, so Daddy and I were two of the four men in my Grandmother's life. My Grandmother did not allow the Christmas Eve meal to be eaten that night, nor a single present to be opened until me and my father arrived home that night. We hung this sow on my Grandparent's front porch where this photo was taken, ate supper, opened presents, then skinned and freezered, this hog. The art of being a good wife, mother, and Grandmother is almost a thing of the past. I have such a wife and am blessed beyond measure to be able to say so, but this above photo is a tribute to my Grandmother Agnes Rosemary Kemmer.

Jack came down for a visit at Christmas and brought us a replacement. It was a full brother to Slim, just a younger litter. His name was Baby Boy. On December 24, 1987 we struck out for the West Pearl for his first hunt. An old football buddy of mine named Brent Craig was in for the holidays from bootcamp for the 82nd Air Bourne, and joined us. LE bayed a big monster sow about 400 pounds and Baby Boy drilled her as soon as he laid eyes on her. She was so big, and we had a little room in the freezer, so we killed her in the woods. Carrying dead weight is much easier than carrying live weight, but it was fun watching Brent take his turn. Daddy and I were well used to this kind of activity, but we teased Brent about that pansy military conditioning he had because he damn near passed out before we got to the boat. Brent was a good tough old boy however, and rolled right along, tired or not.

82nd Airborne member Brent Craig fresh out of Boot Camp having his milk checked in the Swamps of the West Pearl River in Louisiana. My father always said that his Boot Camp experience was like a big playground in the early 60s and was just plain fun. Daddy always said that the only people that viewed Boot Camp as tough were those not raised doing tough things. Brent had just completed Boot Camp, but was not in shape for this. Brent was game however, and though his conditioning was not up to snuff, his mind held out fine.

On January 23, 1988 Baby Boy would get tested on a big Boar, again in the West Pearl. LE would bay in a big fine briar patch and Baby Boy would bolt in. He initially caught a small hog that began to squeal. I shot in the briar patch towards him mostly on my hands and knees down a small pig trail. I was about 30 yards from the squealing pig when off to my left I heard a big Boar approaching, woofing with every breath. Just like hogs from the old stock law days, this Boar had heard the squealing distress call and was on his way. I got extremely still and the Boar came within about 8 feet of me on his way to the Battlefield. He began warping the ground with Baby Boy and cutting him all to pieces. Some how he got Baby Boy off that pig, so Baby Boy then caught him for his trouble. It was fantastic. He was a 'sho nuff' fine Boar.

Crawling through the thicket for this boar puts me in mind of a question that I have often been asked, "Do you crossbreed your catch dogs with other breeds?". The answer

(All 3 photos to right) January 23, 1988. This was Baby Boy's first real test. This Boar came boiling into the briar patch right by me on his way to Baby Boy as he had a smaller hog caught. He put a good slashing on Baby Boy, then got caught and tied, and victory was ours.

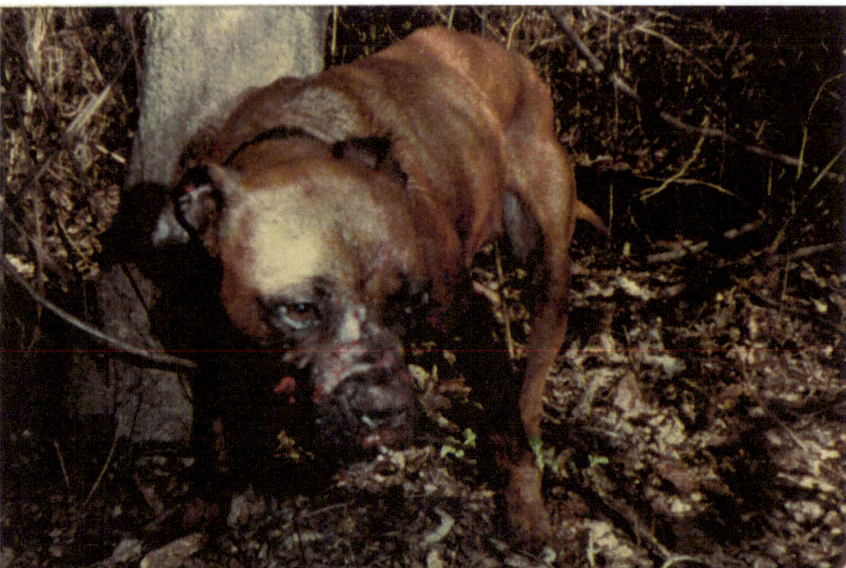

is Never. I know that hog hunters all over the country cross different breeds trying to create the single super dog. We never did that. First, I have been a breeder of animals my whole life and the main thing to know about breeding is that "SHIT FLOATS".

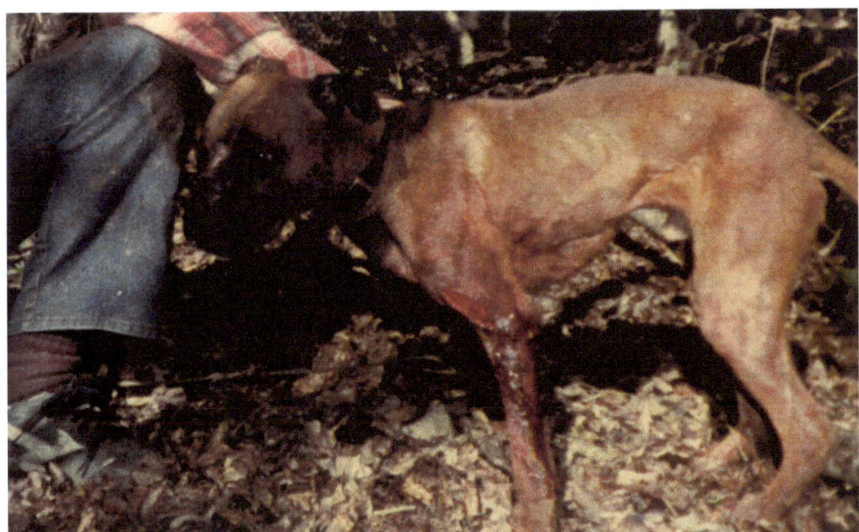

For example men think that breeding animals is like baking a cake, I'll just slip a dab of bulldog in there for grit, a dab of hound in there for a cold nose, a dab of cur in there to make him silent trailing, etc. They have this fairy tale idea that they themselves through 'wish' can determine the exact single trait, out of a thousand, that they want each animal to contribute. Well news flash cake bakers, it don't work like that. The Shit Floats statement means that what you will most likely end up with is the worst possible trait each animal you mix into your trait has to offer. Instead of the toughness of the bulldog, you will get his poor nose. Instead of the silent trailing of the cur, you will get his toughness. Plainly put one more time Shit Floats, it is the worst traits that tend to come to the top. Genetics is a tricky thing. Keep your catch dogs pure American Pit Bull Terrier. We tried Boxer crosses which produced a grouchy cur. We tried english / Pit crosses which caused a slow, gaudy, big chest target, slobbering fat boy that causes too much noise and is not nearly as game. We tried it all and settled on pure Pit Stock bred for gameness. When I am crawling up that pig trail on my hands and knees with no tree close by, I don't want some cross bred trash holding literally my life in his mouth. I want something holding that Boar that has been pure bred for 500 years to take his death with welcome. I want a dog who his direct decedents had there legs chopped off by their owners during the 'Bull Baiting' days of kings, to prove that their blood was acceptable for a pedigree. I want a dog that is bred to welcome death, and has not been watered down by some idiot trying to create a Bay and a Catch dog. We want our bay dogs to bay so we can locate the battlefield, and we want our catch dogs to catch when they arrive and die for me if need be.

This Blurry action shot was of a Kemmer dog and a fine Boar on the Pearl River. Thinking back on my childhood, the Mighty Pearl is the River that runs through my Memory.

Same goes for over training a dog. We had a friend in Picayune Mississippi that trained his catch dogs to release a hog and back off when he ordered them to. Now it was cool as heck to watch. He would grab a back leg, then order his catch dog to back off. The dog would then release the hog, step back about 5 feet, and this guy would deal with the hog. Now there are some very fine benefits to this kind of training. This would have been easy to teach a frequently hunted dog like Speck or Slim, but mine and Daddy's thought process always was that we wanted to physically break them off. The reason was very simple, a battle scene is full of rough stuff, guts getting cut out, limbs being broken, it is a confusing situation to say the least, and we did not want a dog to misunderstand a command and turn loose at the wrong time. Let's say I hollered something to Daddy and the Boar was slinging the catch dog around. One can easily see the room for a misunderstanding by a badly beaten down dog. No we wanted to break him off ourselves.

Now as for bay dogs, many hog hunters want a good rough dog. They believe that if he is rough enough he can stop a hog from running. Well I think we have covered that a hog stops if he wants to. Myself I like a light touch bay dog. For one thing, by not diving in until the catch dogs arrive he lives a lot longer. Silent trailing is a must of course, but when he bays I actually want him backed off a bit, and not so aggressive. I do not want him pressuring an already nervous hog into breaking before the cavalry arrives. Stand back about 5 or so feet and seem to him to be just an aggravating noise that has just awoken him, instead of a full on threat that will panic him into a race. Each man has his own ideas but I have a lifetime of experience and the number of victims we stacked up each year were usually more than double and triple what any competitors that we knew of stacked up. So the proof, as they say, is in the pudding.

As for a specific breed of bay dog we did not have one. Good bay dogs are where you find them. Blackie looked like something you might see hanging around a bunch of dumpsters. If anyone had seen LE they would have put him down out of mercy. He had the Blue Mange from his shoulder blades straight down the middle of his back to the base of his tail, and looked like 'Death eating a Cracker'. Blackie was twice the dog LE was and I never saw another dog that could hold a candle to LE. LE was a straight out asshole who hated all other dogs. Our nickname for him was "Lonely Boy" or "Lonely Parker"(since he came from LE Parker). Also LE stunk to high heaven. On cold days after he got real old we would allow him to ride in the cab of the truck with us and when he would Fart, we damn near had to evacuate the truck. He was the nastiest little dog I have ever been around, but he could flat find a hog. No other pure bred dog that I have ever seen in my life could out locate LE, and Blackie was twice that good. We had a lot of Southern Black Mouth Curs, Catahoula Curs, Kemmer Stock Curs, and they found a few hogs because they covered so much ground they stepped on them. But they did not trail them up and surgically locate them, and they damn sure were not able to count them like Blackie did many times. Most of the hogs I saw pure bred curs find, we would have found in another 5 minutes with a good working crew of catch dogs running loose. So again, good bay dogs are where you find them. Get one, and if he is what I am talking about, unless you lose him, he will last you a good 10 years like LE did us.

Mitch Kemmer in the back carrying a hog. Norman Kemmer in front of him carrying another hog. This photo shows how we carried hogs out on our shoulders alive. With the proper carrying technique done with the head hanging over the back, the hog can not bite or cut the hunter in the back. This hunt was on Horn Island, but not the day of the Storm.

Populations of hogs after our return to the woods would always be fragile. No large numbers that existed in the early 70s would ever be seen again. We struggled to find more places to hunt, as to keep from pressuring any place too much. We were always looking to add a new place to our rotation. This West Pearl area was one of those. As you cross into Louisiana on the I-10 bridge from Mississippi, you cross several Swamps that make up the Pearl River. One is Honey Island Swamp and the other is Devil Swamp. We had hunted them all in the early 70s. In the old days there used to be a legend of what was called the "Honey Island Swamp Monster". Articles in papers were written on him and boogie men hunters always spoke of him. Well Daddy and Jack frequented those woods in the old days, and their belief was that someone saw them carrying out a live hog on their shoulders and that's where the legend started. Also one of the guys that hunted with them in those old days was a man named Drew Favre. Yes this was Brett Favre's cousin. Now Drew was poor in those days and he hunted those deep river swamps with Daddy and Jack barefooted. Yes Barefooted. They figure that someone found old Drew's tracks in there and that helped the Swamp Monster idea even more.

This West Pearl River hunting was near Honey Island and Devil Swamps. Later we would catch a big pregnant Blue colored sow in that swamp with Baby Boy and LE. She was so fine and we wanted to save her, but she could not be tied nor carried on anyones shoulders in her pregnant state. So we remembered a story that my grandfather used to tell. He said when he was a boy and they caught a big hog that they wanted to get home, but did not want to carry, they 'walked him out'. The idea was to tie a string around one back foot. Get a good stout stick in one hand and hold the foot string with the other. Tap them to go, and if they spin on you, jerk the string up, causing the hog to slam to the ground. Soon they will stop that. Then tap to go, and if you want them to go to the right stick the stick in right at the base of their left ear. To go left, stick the base of the right ear. It sounds ridiculous, and yes it would not work on the Red Gap Boar or any other supremely mean hog, but I now know that it will work on most. We always laughed when Pa would talk about it, but buddy we walked this sow about 100 yards and she was taking commands like a seasoned pro. Barely touch her left ear and she would turn right and the same with the left turn. Again Chimpanzee and Dolphin smart. She even got to the point to where when she went in something thick Daddy would drop the rope, let her walk through it, and pick the rope up on the other side. It shocked us both, but we smooth walked that big sow over a mile to get to the river bank. We had a friend in Lafayette Louisiana named Calvin Boutte and he had been asking us for a few hogs to stock an Island he hunted on the Sabine River. So we brought this fine bred Blue Sow to him, and years later we hunted on that same Island catching some of her descendants, no doubt.

What a fine Possum Blue Sow. This is the pregnant sow that we led out of the Swamp and then delivered to an Island on the Sabine River. Here she is one legged to a tree before we began our journey out that day.

Then on September 17, 1988 it was back to Bogalusa with our crew and Baby Boy would catch another fine Boar. We went into the Forks again seeking death. Now Baby Boy was not a talented catch dog, he caught what he got to first and held on. A good talented catch dog can get where ever he wants, and on a hog that is usually the ear. When LE bayed in the forks that day Baby Boy ran in and the first thing he come to was a big nut sack, and he caught it. As I came rolling in it was good open woods and this Boar was looking right at me. Forward he came with Baby Boy hanging off his nuts digging his feet into the earth to try and stop him. I began darting around the Boar trying to get my usual back leg. As Daddy arrived and saw the situation we began our usual routine in a case like this, one tries to get his attention while the other grabs for a leg. Well he had zeroed in on me apparently blaming me for the pain in his private area. Daddy soon got a leg and we got him tied. This catch had a special meaning that day because it was the Boar that had killed Slim. He had been in the back of our minds all morning. Having to watch him walk off after killing Slim never set right, and on this morning we had righted a wrong.

September 17,1988. This is the Boar that killed Slim. With Baby Boy's 'nut sack' catch on him it was a wild ride to get hands on him. This is one of many boars that we floated out of the swamp.

Now this was a big Boar about 260 pounds and too big for our usual shoulder carry, but the swamp was wet that day and there was a slue near by that led to the river about a half a mile away. We then decided to 'float' him out. Floating a hog is like floating a person in a swimming pool. That person is usually too heavy to hold in your arms on land, but you can stand in a pool and hold them up in front of you with ease because they are floating to a large degree. He was tied and I just walked with him in my arms and kept his head above water. Now at spots the slue would be shallow and I would simply drag him across the shallow spots to deeper water. Now many of the bottoms of slues on the Pearl had fresh water clam shells in them. While dragging this boar across one shallow spot the clam shells apparently cut the tie string. Well I had him between my legs sliding him forward, and all of a sudden he just stood up. I quickly got a back leg and called for Daddy who was leading the catch dogs down the bank of the slue beside me. We retied him and away we went. Baby Boy had put some heat on his nuts, and as he stood quickly in that slue, he paid me back a bit by racking mine.

Later on came Baby Boys last day in the hog woods. Some farmers had called us from McNeil Mississippi and wanted us to come after a single hog. Wild hogs did not frequent their little farming community, but one big hog track had appeared up there and was wrecking the corn crop in that area. They said this hog had eluded other hog hunters they had called and they had heard that we could catch anything. The track was enormous and being a single hog in the middle of no where we figured it was an old boar off ranging and had located this honey hole for food. After about a two hour hunt that morning LE bayed and Baby Boy rolled out. I quickly broke for the area of the bay. As I arrived there was nothing. LE was quiet so we knew Baby Boy was there, but there was no site nor sound of them and I knew I was right on top of where the bark came from. Daddy arrived and we agreed to split up quickly and search. After bolting to the right, and Daddy to the left, I began to see blood. Not wanting to holler at Daddy and risk spooking what was a monster track apparently dragging 39 pound Baby Boy away like a rag doll, I just kept trailing. Ahead of me I could see the ass end of this gigantic hog. Not being able to see dogs anywhere I slipped up and grabbed a back leg. As I rose up with the back leg to where I could see the hogs front end I realized that it had Baby Boy in it's mouth and was chewing on him. He appeared to be dead as he lay there limp and lifeless. After grabbing the leg I began to call Daddy. The hog, which had paid me little attention up until now, turned loose of Baby Boy and began turning to try and get me. See a hogs spine is ridged and stiff, and once you have the back leg they can not ball up on you like say, a cat. As the hog turned towards me and dropped Baby Boy, Baby Boy then opened his eyes and drug himself to follow it's front end. He then caught the hog on the foot in his limp and lifeless state. What a fine boy he was. Later we would realize that the hog had broken his spine and he was paralyzed. Whether from warping him around trees, or trying to eat him, his spine had been severed and he would never use his back end again, but by God he had that foot. Now damn it that's a bulldog and you don't water that down with nothing else.

As Daddy arrived we tied this monster which turned out to be a 500+ pound sow. She had apparently escaped from some farmer when she was a pig. She was all white except for two big black spots right between her ears. She was one mean heifer and according to the land owner had eluded at least 7 other crews of hog hunters that he had after her. She ended Baby Boy's hog hunting career on the morning of February 4, 1989.

Earlier we discussed catch dogs and bay dogs, but we also need to touch on men. No man should ever release a bulldog on anything unless he is as tough as he asks his dog to be. That dog will need help on a mature boar. Without it he will be killed. All my

February 4, 1989. This is the Huge Sow from McNeil Mississippi that ended Baby Boy's career in the hog wood.

life I have heard of men climbing trees and watching there bulldog get killed because they did not feel the hog was secure enough for them to move in. Well if you do not have the balls to 'Move In' and help your dog then don't ever turn him loose. Also know that as I right this paragraph, I do it with my teeth gritted, and am trying to watch my language. Man up, or stay on the couch where you belong. Dog hunting for hogs and bringing them out alive is not for the faint-hearted.

Chapter 11
The Mighty Ottis and We Roll On

Contrary to a popular American Myth, not all men are created equal, and as we have discussed neither are all dogs. I would finally be graced by God with the finest catch dog I would ever own. He was the caliber of Hud and Judge. It was now 1988 and we had not seen one like that since 72. His name was Ottis. I had entered another dog sport with my father at this point. The Macho dog earlier spoken of was the absolute best producing male I had ever seen. After his passing we began to breed to his son Bo Bo who was Speck, Slim, and Baby Boys daddy. Recently we had begun breeding to a full brother to Bo Bo named Pistol. One of the very first breedings we made with Pistol was to a daughter of Bo Bo named So. This first Pistol / So breeding produced a fine litter of combat material. I was given one pup off that litter for myself. He was mostly red with some white around his head and neck area and I named him Ottis. I intended him for this other sport, but we always believed that hog hunting a dog when he was young was very good for his overall development. After all hunting is a dogs primary instinct.

We had collected some hogs at a friends house in Alabama and went to pick them up. We did not have any hog trailers so we engineered a top for the bed of our truck much like the tops folks travel with today. A crude plywood set up, but it worked. As we lowered the tailgate of the truck we had fashioned a small door. We went over in January of 1989 and got these hogs. Upon arriving home the fun part began as to how to get these hogs out of the back of this truck and over into my pen. Usually hogs we brought home were tied up, but these 9 Boars were all free in the bed of this truck, under our plywood top. We liked trying new dogs on catches at the house like this but there was a right and wrong way to start a young dog. Usually in starting young dogs we turn a small hog loose in a field, catch him with an experienced dog, and allow the young dog to assist. My father believed in taking all the proper steps to start a dog as not to mess him up when he is young. I myself, becoming known around the house for my bold and blunt opinions due in part, to a speech I was given in the back of a van one night as I sat and cried with my father over the death of a brindle female named Matilda, believed that a good dog could not BE messed up. In fact if he could be 'messed up' I did not want him anyway. Now Daddy had several young dogs at the time that he wanted to start on hogs, but not by carrying them off the chain for the first time in their lives, bringing them to the back of a pick up truck, dropping the tailgate, and shoving them into a dark hole with 9 mature boars in it. He felt this would be a suicidal way to start a young pup. I only had one pup at the time that I wanted to start on hogs, and I was convinced that this was just the way I wanted to start him. Plus, I had spoken to an 'Ole Preacher' one time about gameness and how a dog should act under any circumstances. Against a hale of Daddy's protests I broke to get Ottis.

Now the plan was to bring this young pup up to the tailgate, drop it quickly, shove him in, and close it back. I had a collar on him with a 15 foot lead rope on it. After he caught this would give me a way to pull him to the back of the truck bed, where we would then drop the tailgate and pull him out hog and all. Then we would repeat the process again and again. Now this would have been rough on a grown dog who was seasoned, but this young Ottis pup had never even left the pen he was raised in. As I got him to the back of the truck, Daddy looked at me and said, "This is a Mistake". Now I had a habit of getting a little wild eyed in combat situations, so with my crazy eyes I looked at him and said, "Drop the Tailgate". He then dropped the tailgate, I shoved Ottis in this dark hole, and the tailgate was quickly slammed shut. One fraction of a second and that lead rope took off like a fishing line that had been hit by a big Marlin. The rope took the hide right off the inside of my hands. The entire truck then began to shake violently. I then began pulling the lead rope, bloody hands and all, towards me. Daddy dropped the tailgate and I pulled Ottis out with the first Boar. After penning him we repeated the process. After that first catch there was no split second before take off any more. He knew something was in there now. I would see Ottis do many unbelievable and incredible things in his short life but none topped this day. He caught all 9 boars, just as fast as we could pen one and shove him back in that dark hole. Daddy was right, it was unfair to a young pup and not the right way to begin a catch dog, but on that day I did just the wrong thing with just the right dog. Daddy and I would use the words 'Magic' to describe Ottis for the rest of our lives, but it was whispered first on this cold January day that we brought this young pup out of his pen for the very first time.

Mitch and Norman Kemmer with Ottis. Our truck is parked to the left, just out of the photo. This was the very first Boar Ottis caught. We shoved him into the bed of that dark truck, and this was the first one that we pulled him out with. What a fine pup he was, perfect in all weathers.

Baby Boys death in early February caused us to bring Ottis to the woods for the first time on the 27th of that month. We tried a couple of other older dogs, in weeks prior with no satisfaction. So on this day we took Ottis as our only catch dog to the West Pearl River for his debut. We led him with a chain on that day because he seemed to want to kill LE. Normally when we want to go through the whipping of a new catch dog, we want to do it with another bulldog, because bay dogs are fragile. Plus the damage done to the nine boars Ottis had caught a few weeks before seemed a bit excessive. Two had broken shoulders, and another had a broken front leg. He had caught two in the back legs, and they could not walk. Not broken, but they were blackish purple and useless. So Ottis was showing a degree of power seldom seen, and that is a statement coming from two men that had seen more power than most. So to keep LE safe Ottis stayed on a chain.

We had been seeing some old sign in the swamp that day and were walking in an old dried up pond bed, when LE shot up the bank and bayed about 100 yards from us. I did not want to top the bank with Ottis for fear of spooking the Boar. LE seemed to be bayed good and solid, so I took the chance of releasing Ottis who was pulling towards the barking even though he had never heard a bay dog bark before in his life. By releasing him while still in the pond bed, only his little 36 pound body would pop up over the bank. I released him, paused for a few seconds, heard the catch, and bolted up over the bank myself to as cool a sight as I had ever seen. It was a big beautiful Russian colored Boar. Ottis had hit him face on and had him caught by the bottom lip, the Boar was shaking as violently and crazy as I have ever seen a Boar act in my life. It was like he was on Crack and was spazzing out. He was slinging Ottis from side to side and the Boars bottom lip seemed to be stretched at least a foot. As I ran towards them I never saw Ottis's feet touch the ground and the Boar was slinging him so hard that Ottis would hit the Boar's left side, and then be slung until he hit the Boar's right side. The ferocity and insane intensity of this Boar was incredible. Ottis' feet never touched the dirt until I grabbed this Boar's back legs and lifted them both off the ground. As Daddy arrived and tried to grab Ottis and break him off, the Boar's wild insane attitude continued, and Daddy kept hollering, "Hold him, be sure you're a hold of him". I kept yelling, "I've got him. I've got him". After Daddy got Ottis off it was like trying to hold on to a wild cat. Even though it was February it was a hot day and this Boar's insane struggling and fighting had him extremely hot, so we decided to one leg him to a tree. Tying all four feet together when they are extremely hot will sometimes kill them. So we one legged him to get him to calm down and thus cool off. We had not passed water in some time and the swamp was bad dry. Many times if a Boar gets hot and we can get to water we will cool him with that. As we got him 'one legged' he continued to go crazy. Running at us, and the dog even though we had backed off almost 100 yards or so away. He then began circling the tree, then got twisted up in the tie rope, and began to lunge towards us again and we heard a big 'Pop'. He had broken his own back leg.

LE had left as soon as we broke Ottis off and about that time he bayed. Ottis was still focused on this Boar in front of us. Once a catch dog focuses on a hog he has caught, it is hard to get his attention away. I then grabbed Ottis up in my arms and said with an intense voice, "Listen. Listen.". He then got real quiet, heard LE bark about a half a mile away and began to struggle to get out of my arms pulling towards the bay bark. Confident that he was focused on LE, I took a chance and released him. Daddy, fearing he might

return to this battle site decided it best to wait there until he heard him catch. I, on the other hand, was right behind that little hog catching machine. Apparently the Boar had been there with about an 80 pound sow, and it was her that LE had located. Ottis drilled her like a seasoned pro, and she was ours as well. Now speaking of seasoned pro, this trick I did of picking Ottis up as he was focussed on one animal and getting him to go to a bay bark and leave a hog he

February 27, 1989. This was Ottis' first trip to the hog woods. This Boar was the most insane and intense that I personally have ever had my hands on. At this point in our lives my father trusted me in the hog woods as much as I trusted him, but while breaking Ottis off that stretched out bottom lip he kept hollering to me, "Hold him. Now be sure and hold him". When Norman Kemmer showed concern in combat you know the situation was hot.

could actually see, was amazing. We had only had two or three dogs over a lifetime of hog hunting that we could ever get to do this, and that was always after fooling with them on 50 or more catches. Only the very, most seasoned, of catch dogs would do this, and Ottis did it on his first trip to the woods. Not even Judge could ever be taught to do that. With a live hog in site of him, most bulldogs will not change their focus. When I told Ottis to listen, it was like we had done it 100 times. Daddy and I had seen a lot, but never anything quite like Ottis.

Upon returning to the one legged Boar he was still in the same 100 miles and hour mode. We then decided to tie him and break for the river to cool him off. We made it about 1/4 of a mile and he died from being over heated. Now I have went on and on about how amazing Ottis was on that day, but I also have never seen a Boar this insane in my life. Even the Red Gap Boar and the Rhinoceros Boar were not this intensely crazy acting. This Boar never cut Ottis, this Boar did not kill anything, so I try not to rank him among the bad ones but I will say that if he had had some normal dogs on him and I had not arrived seconds after the catch to get him off balance, this dude was something special. I hated that he lost his life, but at least it was in honorable combat against an honorable opponent.

Kemmer's Ottis' first Boar after he was hog tied. We could never get him to calm down and he died shortly after this photo was taken due to over heating.

During this time of having Ottis we had an interesting occurrence. Now over the years we would have some hog hunter that had a Boar that he would bet us we could not catch with dogs. Of course then we would bet him any money that he wanted to, then catch the

Boar, take the money, and we were all the better for it. Now we could catch any hog with just one of our average, or below average, catch dogs. To suggest, or bet, otherwise was a joke. But during this time when we had Ottis we had a friend in the dogs that had Ostrich's. We were at his house one night and were looking at a big male Ostrich that he had that was about 9 feet tall. He then made some comment to Daddy about what that Ostrich would do to a dog, and it eventually turned into wanting to bet us that we could not catch that Ostrich with one of our dogs. Now had this happened with a dog like Speck or Slim that would have been a joke, but Ottis was the best dog I had ever seen. As I realized what the conversation had turned into, my 'battle eyes' began to glow and I proceeded to try and set the date and the amount of the wager. My mistake was seeming so eager, and he eventually refused to see it through. He gave us the big story of them gutting Lions and all that jazz. What a joke, that little speed demon Ottis would have been attached to that Bird in a split second, but the old boy lost his nerve.

This is me and Daddy catching a hog near home with Ottis. Norman Kemmer on the hogs back legs, and Mitch Kemmer breaking off Ottis. We used what was called a 'Breaking Stick' to pry the dogs mouth open. And no Pit Bulldog's jaws do not 'lock'. That is a myth derived only because they are so determined and hard to break off once they are attached. Ottis was the single hardest dog I ever broke off of anything. His Jaw Power was incredible, just ask LE as he limps by you in the swamp. Ottis' loss was terrible as I had a score to settle with him in another sport. Due to his death that debt never got paid. I am not the type of man that easily accepts an outstanding debt.

Ottis was amazing at everything. We were hunting the swamp one day with him and got into some high water. In high water the snakes tend to get into the tree limbs to help float out the water. As I was walking in the water on this day I saw a cotton mouth in a tree limb. The water was about two foot deep and Ottis was walking beside me. Now one thing that we used to do when dogs became more and more seasoned in the woods was teach them that if we grabbed them and picked them up, they were to learn that we were pointing them at something in particular. Often when hunting the hunter may be able to see something in the distance that a dog does not. By being able to physically point the dog, he can zero in on it. A very seasoned dog at this art of pointing will, when picked up, simply look straight ahead. This allows the hunter to do the actual pointing, instead of the dog moving his head looking for the object. So the more seasoned, the more the dog froze in place when picked up, and just looked straight in the direction he was being pointed. On this day with Ottis and the Cotton Mouth, when I picked him up he froze in a full alert mode and stared straight ahead, just like he had done it a thousand times before. I then pointed him at the snake. As soon as he saw it, I leaned him forward enough to catch it, and he did. Now when a dog catches a snake, his goal is to violently shake it to death. He will go into a shaking frenzy the likes of which you have never seen. This shaking is crucial because the quick side to side shaking keeps the snake from biting him as he shakes it to death. A talented snake killer is like a talented anything else. Also this snake killing shake is as much an instinct to a dog as where he catches certain animals. Mother Nature provides this instinct and talent depends on how good he is at it. Ottis was a snake killer, like he was everything else, he was the best I ever saw. Now I never passed a Cotton Mouth in the woods and left it alive, but I also knew that by pointing Ottis to this snake in two foot of water that it would not allow him to do his much needed shake to kill it. So I held him up above the water for the shake. Now this showed my confidence in this dog. This was the very first snake he had ever seen, and I was going to trust that he was talented enough to shake him to death in such a mad fury that neither Ottis or me, being so close, would get bit. Knowing how Ottis had conducted himself in every other regard when it came to talent, I had all the confidence in the world. Of course he killed the snake, and as he was killing it and I turned my head when the thrashing got to a fever pitch, I saw a second snake in a tree just to my right. As soon as the shaking was done, I spun Ottis, snake still in his mouth and pointed him to the second snake. He then dropped the first and grabbed the second and the killing continued. When he was done with that one I had a funny feeling that we had waded into a snake infested area, so I stood and looked around before setting Ottis down. Sure enough about 10 feet from me I saw a third snake. We then killed it as well. His first time to see a snake in his life and we kill three in a matter of two minutes as I held him. It had something to do with the word 'magic'.

Ottis's next trip to the woods was to the Pascagoula for a flood hunt. It had set in a week long heavy rain so we headed to the swamp for a 'Search for High Ground' hunt. We only brought Ottis, because if we found high ground everything would be there and no bay dog would be needed. Now this swamp provided some well known high ground spots that we could get to with the boat. Daddy would drop me and Ottis on one end and pick us up on the other end. Well about the third one we hit, it was covered with hogs. Ottis shot into the thicket and the woods erupted with movement and hog woofing. As I ran in a trail a big Boar met me running out. Then as I got in site of Ottis I saw at least 30 hogs covering him up. That old protection instinct was in full force on that small piece of ground. I began kicking and pushing my way through hogs to get to him. As I reached him he had about a 150 pound sow caught. As I one legged the sow and struggled to get him off for another hit, the hogs on that tiny spot all hit the water and swam for it. By the time I got him broke off they had all cleared out.

All in all we hunted Ottis a total of four times and caught 8 hogs with him in the woods. I was never around a better snagger in my life. I saw him go in on the side of a big fallen tree one day because he was winding some hogs. The hogs, lying on the other side of the tree, then bolted out and me and Daddy said, "Damn he went to the wrong side". About that time he came backing out of the briars with a sow he had somehow squeezed under the log and caught. Several times Daddy and I would release him to LE bayed way off and he would arrive so fast we could not believe it. Hud, nor Judge had ever covered ground like he did. He was outstanding. Once we released him to a bay bark by LE on the edge of a big body of water and when Ottis got there the hogs had hit the water. LE was still standing at the water's edge when Ottis got there, he looked around and saw no hogs, so he caught LE instead. We were within sight of him when he caught LE and broke him right off, but that small pinch crippled LE for life. We hunted with him for at least another 5 years and he was never right again. We called it "The Ottis Limp". Ottis would be killed in a Kennel Accident at our home on June 15, 1989. He was still just a pup, but what a pup he was. I had been hog hunting for a couple of years since the death of Speck and Slim, but my whole heart was not in it. Ottis, and our brief time with him, had gotten me all excited again, but the moment couldn't last.

LE in his lifetime with us in the hog woods would turn out to be a strange, odd, quirky, but fine little bay dog. He was always a little shy and spooky and would only allow me and Daddy to touch him. In the woods he was deathly afraid of the bulldogs, due to incidences like the one that caused the 'Ottis Limp', but in truth he was like this all his life, way before Ottis pinched him. Dogs have different personalities just like people, and all in all LE was an asshole. Speck and Slim grew to love, respect, and count on LE, but no matter how much they tried to befriend him, he would not give them the time of day. He stayed primarily under our feet in the woods. When we would hunt with other hog hunters, who had heard what a great location dog LE was, they would watch him under our feet and look at each other with disgust, but soon he would slip away and locate hogs that their bumbling curs never knew were in the area. If we were in a place where we had gotten a false report of hogs, and LE got bored he might disappear. Thinking he might be after a hog, me, Daddy, and the catch dogs would set down and wait for him. Then without hearing even a breaking branch, we might look over and see him laying near us eating a rabbit that he had slipped off and

(Top) Mitch Kemmer and Kemmer's Ottis in Tennessee shortly after my Grandparents moved back there from Mississippi. I was prepping Ottis for a Massacre on a debt at this time. His kennel accident that took his life was not long after this. This photo taken in late March in the snow of Tennessee was the last photo of Ottis.

(Bottom) Mitch Kemmer with Ottis and Norman Kemmer with LE after a nice hunt on the Pearl.

caught. He would never make a sound, disappear, run a rabbit down and catch it, then slip back up, find us and lay down to eat his catch. He was the fastest dog I had ever seen in my life. Even Ottis, who had blinding speed beyond comprehension, could not outrun LE. I often commented to my father that I would like to see LE in a race with a Greyhound, just so I would know how fast a Greyhound could run. I knew it would not outrun LE, but it would give me a point of reference.

When baying or running hogs we also noticed the strangest things with him. We have seen him bay a hog, it break and run, and LE come back to us in 2 minutes. Other times I have seen him run a hog for over 4 hours and it finally bay up. Daddy and I began to believe that LE knew which ones would never bay, and which ones would. Now most that read those last few sentences will laugh and write him off as lazy, but Daddy and I believed our theory so much that we began to never question LE's judgment on such things. Often we would hunt with other hog hunter's and their dogs. Once while hunting with Ronnie Amacher of Picayune Mississippi, LE slipped off and bayed before any of the other bay dogs. When Ronnie's curs arrived the hog broke. LE soon returned to us and Ronnie looked at us as if he wondered why we kept such a dog. Daddy said, "If LE came back that fast, then that hog will never hold bay". Now Ronnie was one of the best hog hunters we knew. He did not hunt for the 'Fast Break' like we did. His dogs opened on the trail and would run a hog all day. After this hog broke and LE came back Ronnie's dogs then ran him for the rest of the day, only returning empty handed that night, as the hog never stopped running. Meanwhile we went on hunting with LE and the catch dogs that day as Ronnie's dogs could be heard in the distance. We caught two hogs that day with LE, as Ronnie's bay dogs chased a ghost that never decided to stop. It was many days like this that gave us a strange confidence in this little spooky, mangy, strange, stinking, nothing of a dog we called LE.

Ottis had two litter mate brother's that we were eyeballing for the woods. We had broken an unwritten law around our house. If we used a dog name, we would never use it again. But in Ottis' litter for some reason Daddy named a male Judge. Now again this was something that we never ever did, but Daddy broke the rule this one time because this male was identical to the old original Judge dog. Another brother of Ottis' was a dog name Oscar. We had used him for something else so he could never be allowed to run free as a catch dog due to causing trouble but we were desperate so we used him for a while. We were also using a little bitch named Mascara. She was fair and could be left loose to respond to LE on the fly and Oscar had to be sent in after the initial hit, for the real anchor. Oscar was real tough and reliable. It made for a good crew until the next death occurred.

July 14, 1989. Mitch Kemmer with LE and Norman Kemmer with Oscar. Oscar was a litter mate brother to Ottis. This Yamaha motor seen on the back of this boat was the one we bought right after our old Mercury 20 HP died on us after the Horn Island Hurricane hunt.

Brent Craig on the left holding a little Robert T. bred bitch called Fancy (given to me by a good friend named Ken Allen) Fancy was worthless even as a hog dog. Mitch Kemmer on the right holding Mascara, a Kemmer bred bitch. This photo was used by a Hunting Magazine called Full Cry on an article they did not only on Kemmer bred dogs, but also on the hog hunting exploits of Norman and Mitch Kemmer. The article was on our cousin Robert Kemmer and his line of Kemmer Stock Curs that have been in the Kemmer family since 1806. But me and my father were who they used as an example of, in there words, 'Real Hog Hunters' who actually hunted with these dogs.

We had caught several hogs with our new crew and they were working fair together. Again Oscar could not be released until we knew there was a hog there, but if there was he would catch it, instead of the other dogs. Then we hit Diamond Head one day. Populations were thin there and it was a long hard day of marsh and woods hunting, but late that evening LE bayed in a thick Pine Flat. I was leading Oscar and Daddy and had gotten separated on the way to the Boar when I heard Mascara arrive. I knew she had arrived because I heard her start Screaming. She was caught, and the screaming was through her clinched teeth just like Heck on the Red Gap Boar, but she was screaming to a pitch that would make your skin crawl. As soon as I heard it I released Oscar as to send her help as fast as I could. As soon as he got clear of me with his brush breaking I could hear Daddy screaming behind me, "Cut Oscar loose, cut Oscar loose". He had heard Mascara as well. I then Yelled, " He is on his way". Then I rolled forward as fast as I could possibly run. It was thick and I was crawling, running when I could, backing through briar patches, and digging with everything I had to go faster. I do not ever remember trying so hard to cover ground. The next day all the muscles in my stomach were sore. I knew they needed help desperately and I was about to bust to give it to them. All was quiet but I had a direction. All of a sudden I came into a little opening. It was about 20 yards wide and 50 yards long and it was clear all but some sage brush. I saw this as an opportunity to make up some time so I bolted. As I blew through the sage brush I busted right in on the catch without realizing they were that close. I came in face on with the Boar, dogs attached to each ear, and he came at me with his mouth wide open. I was running too fast to stop, so I jumped up and over him to my left. As I went over him I saw him spin with me. I landed in some big Bramble Briars. This is a type of vine type briars that grow up into the trees. They are about 1 inch thick on average and would give the appearance of a rope. Only this rope has large thorns on it. As I landed in them, I grabbed on and began to pull myself up, expecting to get slashed or bit at any point. As I looked back over my right shoulder to assess the Boar's position on me, all I could see was the top of his shoulders. That meant his head was right between

December 19, 1989. The Diamond Head Boar that killed Mascara. I give much respect to him, he was the real thing. From left to right is Norman Kemmer, Jason Tromley, Mitch Kemmer, and Tom Tromley. This was the end of a long and bloody day. As I use to say, "A day without Blood, is like a day without Sunshine".

my legs. Daddy came flying in at that point, and with the Boar facing me, he got a back leg. I then worked quickly around and got the other leg. Daddy said, "How bad did he get you?". I said, "I'm not sure, but I don't think he got me at all". Daddy had entered the clearing just as I jumped over the Boar and had seen it all.

We got the Boar tied and the dogs off and had to go get friends to help us work this 350 pound monster out of the woods that night. He cut Mascara 13 times, Oscar 4 times, and he even cut LE, which never happened. He was accurate, fierce, and deadly. We would rank him among the top 5 baddest that we ever caught, and he deserved it. Mascara would spend the night in my bedroom that night in a dog box. The date was December 19,1989, and it was too cold for a severely wounded dog to be outside. My wife and I laid down for bed about 10 pm. About 10:15 Mascara began a whimpering, quivering, type moan. My wife then said, "I have never heard a bulldog do that before". I asked, "Do you know what she is doing?". She said, "No". I then said, "She is dying". She then asked if I was sure and I responded, "She will be dead in 60 seconds", and she was. I had been around death in the dogs since birth. I knew how rare it was for them to show pain. They took it and welcomed the end, no matter how brutal. That day in the woods was the first, and only time, I had ever heard one scream on a hog like that. It is the rarest sound of all with the bloodline we had. I hated to hear it, I would have given my own life to have been able to get there faster, and I will never forget that sound.

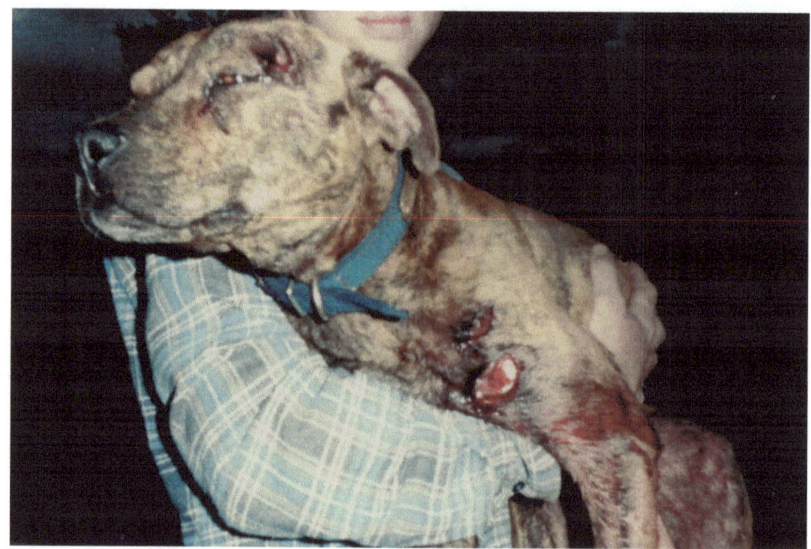

Mitch Kemmer holding Kemmer's Oscar the night we caught the Diamond Head Boar that killed Mascara. Mascara was a fine little gyp, but was screaming while taking her killing. A dog like Oscar does not posses the ability to scream.

Oscar would continue to be as reliable as you could ask for. We were never able to turn him loose with other dogs,

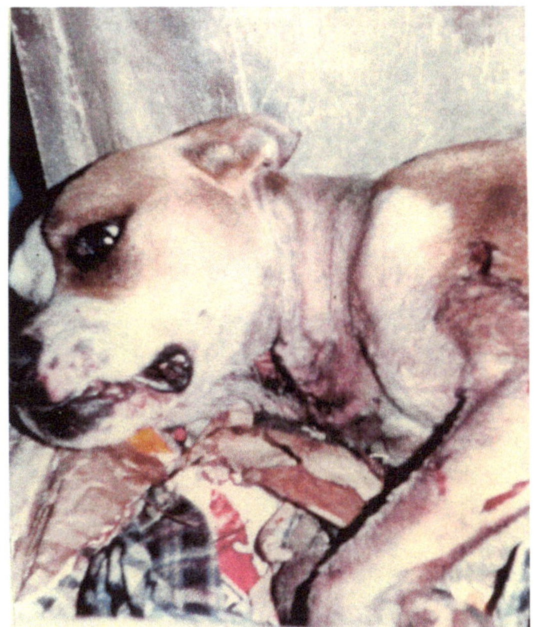

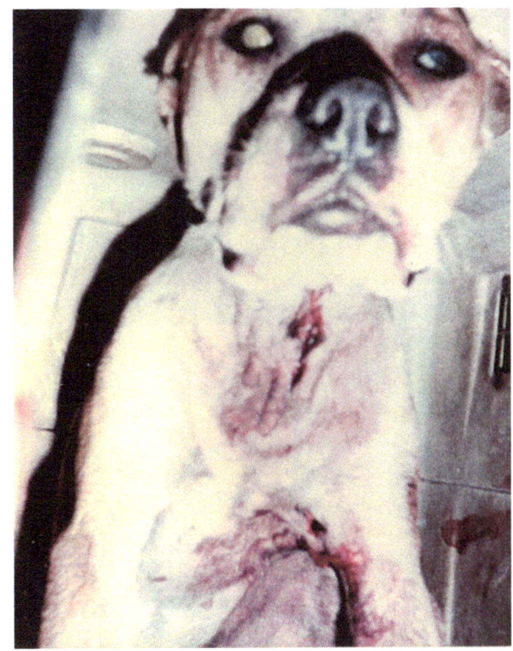

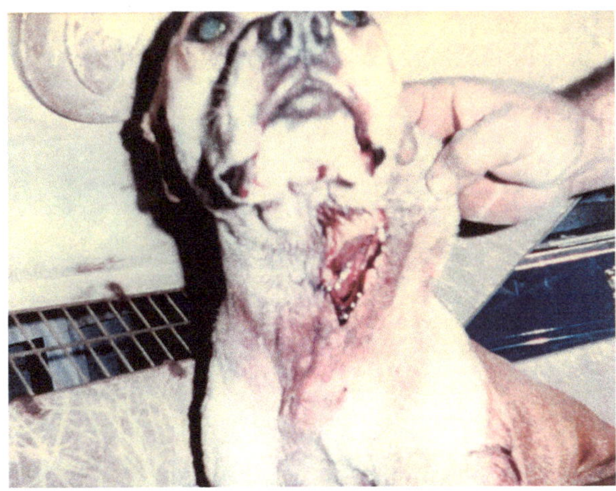

These are photos I took of Mascara after catching the big listed Boar in Diamond Head that night. The cut throat did not hit a main artery. She had several straight in shots, but none hit her heart. We have had many dogs cut more times than her and live, but the brute force with which he was hitting her probably busted her up inside. These photo's were of her in the box in my bedroom that night. When we laid down we knew she would have a tough night, but believed she would live. When that quivering wine started however, I knew she was dying. Her catch was the only time I personally ever heard a bulldog screaming during a catch. It was a shame to lose her, but again 'Death in Combat ……..'

but when you knew there was a hog there and you released him, it was caught. He wasn't an Ottis, but he was a Jakel. The next four years would see us hunting as much as possible, but Oscar's Daddy Pistol was proving to be a good producer and many of his pups were coming of age so we drifted heavily in another sporting direction for a time. We never dropped hog hunting like Daddy and Jack did in the very early 80s with

Pistol's Daddy Macho, but just as good hog dogs would pull a man to love hog hunting like Speck and Slim did, names like Devan and Hank Snow would pull me in another direction. We slowed to hunting when we could.

(Top right) Norman Kemmer to the left holding LE, Tom Tromley in the center, and Mitch Kemmer to the right holding Oscar. This Boar was caught in a wide open field in Robin Wood Forrest in Saucier Mississippi. We spotted him from a vehicle and Daddy told me to take Oscar and run straight to him. When the Boar saw me and broke to run, Oscar saw him. Once a dog like Oscar sees him, it's his ass. Oscar covered two hundred yard before that Boar covered sixty. He mowed him down like short grass. Nothing on this planet is finer than a good bulldog.

September 27, 1990. We had a friend come down from Tennessee to visit us in Mississippi. Daddy was away so me and Oscar took him to the swamp for a quick morning of fun. Above is Mitch Kemmer and Bobby Godsey.

Chapter 12
Death in Battle

In February of 1995 I moved to Tennessee. All my life I had visited here on vacation and loved it. On many trips up we had hog hunted here as well. I began a Brick Masonry business up here, much like Daddy had in Mississippi. I worked my wife and myself through College working for him and as soon as we both graduated we moved. After getting my business rolling good he began coming up and working with me. We then started drifting from Mississippi to Tennessee hog hunting. A good friend of the family named Louie Paull would begin hunting with us a lot during this time. Louie's father Brad was hunting and dogging with Daddy about the time Louie and I were born, so he fit right in. It was in this 95 time frame that I noticed a big change in my father's health.

Hunting with him in Tennessee one day with a pack of my Grandfather's cur dogs we got into some hogs. The Mountains of Tennessee was a far cry from Texas Flat Road in Mississippi and when we got into the hogs I was leading a bulldog that was a little fight crazy. They bayed and I took off, but the hogs broke before I could get close and the dogs were running. So I stopped to wait for a bay bark. Setting for a while on a Mountain ledge, I was expecting Daddy to catch up to me but he never did. I then went back in the direction that I had come from. I found him laying on the side of the Mountain flat on his back. As I rushed up he looked at me. I asked if he was alright and

Three generations of Kemmer's checking out a fine young Boar just caught. From right to left, Norman, Mitch, and Leko Kemmer.

he said he just needed to lay there a minute. I had never seen Daddy go down on a chase like that before. As we sat there together he began to tell me that he had been having some trouble. He described an event he had had in the woods alone a few months earlier. Looking back on it through an adults eyes now I know he had had a heart attack. I asked him about going to the doctor and having it checked. He said he did not want to be cut on and that he believed in doing things the natural way. I also knew that Daddy did not have Health Insurance, nor any money other than the 'week to week' subsistence that a brick mason's life provides, so I knew money was a factor. We came from a family of heart trouble. My Grandfather started a string of surgeries at 55, my uncle Jack had his first Heart Attack at 35, and the future would see my only brother die at 42 from a massive Heart Attack, so it was in the blood. After my brother's death I would go in for a check up and be told that our bodies in my family produce too much cholesterol. The doctor also explained that it was such a production that diet alone would not solve it, so I was put on Crestor to help lower it. So this time was probably seeing my father with several clogged arteries. We would hunt on however, just like a good tough bulldog.

We were hunting in an area in Tennessee one morning with my Grandfather who was living here now as well. He had two rough cur dogs and had heard of some hogs near by. We did not bring a catch dog on this day because Pa was wanting us to do it strictly with his curs. When hunting the mountains for hogs Pa had taught us that in cold weather the hogs would always bed on the South East Side of the mountain. This was to block the cold North wind and also to be in a position to catch the first rays of sunlight in the mornings. Again Chimpanzee and Dolphin smart. Knowing these mountains like the back of his hand, from his childhood, he instructed me and Daddy where to go. Sure enough they bayed in those bluffs.

As we approached from below, we could see two big hogs looking down on us. The curs had them bayed solid and on such a cold morning they were holding tight to their beds. Seeing that these cur dogs were not going to march straight in face on with these two, Daddy told me to climb up on the bluff above them and jump off and catch one. He laughed as he meant it in a joking manner, but off I went. Both hogs looked to be big old sows, and while a sow will hurt you badly, she won't kill you. I then positioned myself right over the two and made about a 12 foot jump and landed right a straddle of one of them. The other broke for the creek below with dogs on her butt. As soon as Daddy and I tied this one, we headed towards the bay bark. As we approached the big black sow was in a creek bed with both sides straight up around her. We devised a plan to situate our selves one up the creek from her and one down the creek from her. On a signal we would both jump in the creek. With walls too steep to climb to her sides she would be forced to run over one of us, then it would be her ass. She chose to charge me, so I got to make the catch. Pa was so high on his two cur dogs that we agreed to tell him that they had caught the hogs. We allowed them to get a bite of both hogs, while tied to give the kindness some validity. All in all it was fun on a nice crisp morning.

Louie called me late one night from Mississippi and his first words were, "Man I almost lost your Dad today in the West Pearl Swamp". Daddy had had a spell and had to lay down for about 3 hours before being able to walk out. When Louie told me I explained to him what had happened on the Mountain Side in Tennessee the year before. We both shared our wishes, but also knew that Daddy was not a man that you could tell what to do. I explained to Louie that either him or me needed to be with Daddy from here on out on every hunt he went on. That way he would not HAVE to do anything if he couldn't. If he was by himself he was going to help his dogs no matter what. His honor and code would not allow otherwise, but if one of us, or better yet, both of us were there, we could handle it by ourselves if necessary. Louie agreed and we did our best to keep up with his movements.

December 26, 1988. These were the sows that Daddy and I caught in Tennessee hunting with Pa's pack of curs. I jumped off the bluff to catch the spotted sow, and Daddy and I surrounded the Black sow in a creek bed. She then charge me and I caught her by hand as well. A nice chilly morning of fun in the Tennessee Mountains and we told my Grandfather that his cur dogs caught them both. He was so proud and confident in them that we wanted him to have bragging rights.

Louie collected a bitch about this time named Lacy. He got her some how through some old woman who had raised her as a house pet. She was pure pit, brindle mostly, with clipped ears, and she was an ace. Her speed, talent, ability, and nose ranked with that of Hud, Judge, and Ottis. Daddy had a couple of catch dogs at the time and was running a Catahoula for the first time named Blue. Louie also had a good Catahoula at the time named Curley. All in all they made for a fine crew. Curley eventually went blind from too much hunting in the Marsh Grass, but we hunted him blind until his death. He could find a hog, even blind. Greg Murray, the guy from the Horn Island hunt, had a younger brother that threw in with us from time to time as well.

Daddy called me one Sunday night and asked me what I was doing that week. Well I was like him, I was on a brick job 5 days a week and was only free on weekends. Knowing that he knew this I asked, "Why what's happening?". He then proceeded to tell me that Louie had made a connection for a hog hunt in Kauffman Texas, just East of Dallas. They were headed that way Monday to hunt on Tuesday. Now Daddy never specifically asked me to go hunting like this. If it was convenient and I was there I went, so this was strange. Following my strict work ethic code I told him I could not

Norman Kemmer holding a freshly caught pig. In front of him is the brindle female belonging to Louie Paull named Lacy. Hud, Judge, and Ottis were the three best catch dogs that we ever owned. This Lacy bitch would be the fourth best catch dog I ever saw.

go. I was bricking the house of a friend of mine Greg Cole at the time. The next morning on the job Greg could tell I was quiet for some reason and asked what was wrong. After explaining it to him, he said, "Put that Trowel down and let's go". Within two hours we were rolling for Texas. Daddy had given me the directions just in case, Ha Ha. So we did not tell him we were coming, neither of us had cell phones even though they existed by now, so we rolled in as they were loading dogs that Tuesday morning. I wouldn't have taken a million dollars for the smile on my father's face as he saw us pull up. He was, and always had been, my best friend in the whole world. I was so glad to make that hunt, knowing he wanted me there.

It was a fine day and we got into hogs from beginning to end. Me and Louie were out front, all day chasing battle sites, and stacking up hogs. One catch caused us to have to swim about a half a damn mile. That guy had a nice spot and we made the most of it. Daddy, Greg, and the land owner would usually arrive as we were finishing the tie job. Louie and I were both young and full of beans and trying to out do each other. The best boar of the day was the last one late in a long hard day. The Bay dogs bayed, the bulldog was released and we rolled out down an old railroad dummy line. As we approached the battle site we could see that the dogs had a big boar caught in the water. As we paralleled them we dropped off the dummy line towards them, me just in front of Louie. As we started off the bank my arm got caught in a big Brahma Briar and it hung me up. Louie passed me and stopped at the water's edge about 20 foot from the hog. The only catch dog we had had caught the hog in the ass and they were in about 3 feet of water. The hog had sat down with the catch dog ahold of his butt, while fighting off the two Catahoula's in his face. Knowing the bulldog was caught these two rough Catahoula's were coming in with a vengeance trying to get a hold. By setting down with the bulldog it put him under water. As Louie hit the water's edge the bulldog popped up and went floating down the slue, and had drowned. Seeing this Louie stopped. As I got loose from my brier I passed Louie hitting the water. Fearing that I had not seen the floating bulldog he hollered, "Wait Mitch, he's not caught". But I had assessed the situation, and saw the floating bulldog, but the Catahoula's had not. They were crowding the Boar hard trying to assist the catch dog that they thought was still in hold, and I hoped that this would hold the Boars attention long enough for me to grab a leg. As I came up behind him and tried for a leg he was still setting down on his butt in that water from the bulldog drowning. So as I felt for a leg that was up under him I had to go down so far that my chin was touching the Boar right between

Kauffman Texas hog hunting trip. This was the big Boar caught in the water at the end of the day. The Catahoula dog in the photo sitting to the far left was Daddy's Blue dog. He died later that night from wounds he took from this Boar.

his shoulder blades. It was a cool little moment that I will treasure, and as I came up with one leg Louie baled in and grabbed the other. We were pulling him up to dry land as Daddy and them approached down the dummy line. Daddy's Catahoula named Blue would die later that night from his wounds. It was a fine battle and a fine Boar.

As we got him tied we assessed our situation and where we could get a truck to load him out. The closest road was over a mile and this Boar was weighing in at about 240. Daddy's deteriorating health over the last 4 years had cut him out of the hog carrying line up and this boar was on the top end of what could be carried. As we stood around him weighing our options, my heart began to break. Daddy was straight across from me in the circle and I was watching him as he looked down at this big Boar. I knew what he was thinking. Someone once asked me why I wore a watch and my answer was, "To keep up with my worst enemy". Father time had broken down the best of men and I knew that my father, in his youth would have carried this Boar out. He was the very best and the very strongest at it that I had ever seen. He was way stronger than me. The land owner suggested Poling him out, other's suggested killing him to lighten the load, as my father stood silent just looking down at him. I then said, "I can carry that hog out". The land owner and Greg both said that idea was crazy. But I had never taken my eyes off my father through the entire conversation. Then he slowly looked up at me and smiled. He said, "Alright". Looking back I know now he had been waiting for me to say it. My father was cold, quiet, and strong, and I rarely felt that anyone impressed him, but I know in that moment he was proud of me.

Now carrying a Boar is a matter of not only strength, but style. He must be positioned on your shoulder as to hang his head straight over your back. If his head is not situated properly he can slice or bite you in the back. The pick up is technique as well. Your strong hand goes way under his front shoulder, your other hand a hold of his back Hock. You then pick up first to your knees for a short pause and a feel for the weight and then the heft up over the shoulder. Now most hogs a man can lift himself, but anything over about 180 or so, it takes some help for the lift. When getting help they will help up and over the shoulder, then allow you to center the weight then the carry is all alone. Anyone walking beside you assisting with the load will only throw you off balance. So on this Texas Boar they helped me up with him. As I shifted the weight to center and prepared for them to give it all to me I only had one thought. I knew that if I carried him Louie would have to try. No one else would even attempt, but if I did it I knew Louie would have to out of honor. Now being the competitors that we were,

Louie Paull, Norman Kemmer, and Mitch Kemmer with the Kauffman Texas Boar right after getting him tied. This was the last Real Good Boar I caught with my father. This is a photo of a good crew, at the end of a good day. This Boar killed two dogs, but one of them was by drowning. I remarked that the Red Gap Boar was the only Boar to ever kill two dogs. That is because I view drowning a dog as 'cheating', but this Boar was a fine challenge.

my thought as they gave me all the weight, was a simple hope that he would be all I could possibly stand, so that it would be too much for Louie. So brother when they let the weight go on my shoulders that hot Texas evening my wish came true. It was a serious load as I began the walk. Now the rules on the carry are simple, you go as far as is comfortable on the first carry, a little further on the second, and more on the third. Never burn yourself out on the first carry. You will find the build up in distance each time will find you in that second wind that few find today. After 5 or 6 carries you will find yourself going 10 times further than the first carry. That first carry for me that evening saw me going about 100 yards, then they helped me down with the Boar. I rested about two minutes and said, "Let's go again". Louie then butted in, as he should, and said, "No, it's my turn". I smiled and said, "Okay". We then helped the Boar up on his shoulders and he got centered and said, "Give him to me". Then he settled the weight, took one step, and his ankle snapped, and he went down in a roll. Now friends love to try and one up one another, especially in the Alpha Male South. So until this day I have enjoyed teasing Louie about the rest of the trip out that night. I would carry that Boar a stretch, then set him down and go back and carry Louie up to him. That broken ankle caused him some grief, but truth be told he was a fine hog hunting buddy to my father and I, and me and him still hunt together today. When I arrived home from that trip I told my wife that I was glad that I went. My exact words were, "If I had not been there Daddy would have died". It was a hard hunt and Louie needed help. My thought was that Daddy would have given it to him, and it would have pushed his clogged arteries too far.

Greg Cole with the Kauffman Texas Boar after we got him out of the woods.

Norman Kemmer at the back of a truck loaded with hogs caught in Kauffman Texas on February 19, 1999.

During this time Louie had developed some friends in Quitman Mississippi, up around Meridian. They were reporting to him that they had recently had an influx of hogs in their area that were not only hitting a few crops, but also their freshly planted food plots. According to them this hog intrusion had been going on and building up for about a year and a half. So when they called we decided to start hitting that place every weekend. Normally we rotated hunting places as to not hit them too hard and consistent so we would not drive the hogs out. The goal in Quitman was to drive them out, so consistent pressure was the key. After hitting that area for about 6 to 8 weeks, as regularly as we could the hogs were gone. Louie and I would speak to those men 16 years later by chance, and they said the hogs never came back into their area. Many say that once hogs infiltrate an area, they cannot be driven out. Well so much for that. We always found that the only way not to drive hogs from any area is not to hunt it very often. Of course that must mean a team of good hunters, with good dogs. Some of those hog hunting crews in South Mississippi hit the Pine Hills area every weekend and there are still hogs there. Even though those guys never seemed to effect the Pine Hills population AT ALL, we only worked Pine Hills into our rotation about every 10 weeks or so. We usually found that when we hunted somewhere, it seemed to make an impact.

Mitch Kemmer with his soon to be wife Joy. The first time I took Joy to Mississippi me, her, and Daddy headed to Bogalusa that first morning to catch a hog. I like to tell folks that this was mine and my wife's first date.

Joy Kemmer, Norman Kemmer, and Louie Paull leaving the Boat Launch for our last hunt with my father.

Mitch Kemmer, Norman Kemmer, and Louie Paull on our last of many, boat rides together.

My next trip to Mississippi took me to a Deer Hunting Camp for a few days and then on down to home. As I arrived my father asked what my plans were for that weekend and I said, "To hunt with you as much as you want to". So the next morning He, I, Louie, and my wife Joy all broke for the West Pearl. The weather was perfect and I did a rare thing that day. I took pictures all day. Normally I only took them of the catches, but that day I photoed the boat ride, the launch, the woods, the catch, and the carry out. I don't know why, but I did. We caught a nice young Boar, and my wife took pictures of me, Louie, and Daddy tying him. We never did that. It was a great day.

(Above) Norman and Mitch Kemmer tying their last hog together, as Louie Paull looks on.

(Right) Mitch Kemmer carrying out alive, the last Boar him and his father caught together.

One night I called him to tell him of the death of one of our favorite combat dogs named Devan. He asked me what I was doing the following weekend. I told him I was having my taxes done, then asked him what was up. He blew it off as just curiosity and said no more. About 10 am that next morning I got a call from Danny Murray. It seems Daddy and Jason Murray had went on a hog hunt, caught a big boar, and after the tie Daddy suddenly fell over dead. It seems that the hunt was being planned when he asked me what I had going. Looking back, if I had been available he would have invited

Louie, Joy, and Norman loading up in the Boat, to head home from the West Pearl.

Women have to take care of the men when they are at home, but good men take care of women when it's time to drag a boat across the shallows. Joy Kemmer enjoys her perch as me, Louie, and Daddy do the hard stuff.

me, but since it was taxes he just chose to play it off. The story I received from Jason was that they caught a big Boar, it killed one dog, and after they got him tied, Daddy stood up and they were joking about calling me and teasing me about what a fine hunt I had missed. Then all of a sudden Daddy froze up, and fell straight back dead. Danny's first version was short and said the they caught a big boar and Daddy died. My first question was, "Did they catch and tie the Boar?". Danny said, "Yes". My plan was to go after him and get him on my way to the funeral if necessary as a matter of honor. But it pleased me to know that my father not only Died in Battle, but he completed the task.

Mine and Louie's plan to stay with him on hunts had failed. See Jason and Louie had been feuding a little over some issues, and apparently Daddy had been hunting with them both. Jason's Daddy Danny had a deer hunting Camp in Ackerman Mississippi and that is where they had gone. It was February 26, 2000. If Louie had not been feuding with Jason, he would have been there. If I had not been having my taxes done, I would have been there. Now our presence may not have made a difference, but I will say that either of us would have needed less help in that desperate situation that Jason would have. I suspect that it got quite intense when that dog got killed, and Daddy had to push, when he probably needed to rest, and those clogged arteries just had all they could stand.

I have made peace with this many years ago and feel about it the same way I did with Speck. Dying in battle covered in blood is so much better than growing old and having to have people watch you lie helpless in a hospital bed. I know what Daddy would have chose if asked. I know what Daddy did choose. Many today have fussed that he did not seek help. Many have fussed at me for not pushing him in that direction. My answer is that I could never see him old. I could never imagine him helpless. Watching him stand in that circle around that Boar in Texas and him not be able to carry him out was the beginning of a slow mental death, and I hurt for him that day more than you can imagine. The only way for a true warrior to die is in combat. I was happy for him. At my end I suspect I will be Jealous. I have lost my finest Comrade. I did not put him in a cemetery with a bunch of lesser clucks. I buried him on the same sacred ground where warriors like Speck, Hud, Judge, Ottis, and Matilda were buried. My bones will be placed beside him when I cross over the river, and I will meet him and Hud on the other side.

The tombstone of Norman Kemmer. One dog sport represented to the left, and a Wild Boar on the right, as my youngest son Norman Mitchell Kemmer III and my oldest daughter Dallas look on. My wife and children have always told me that my life has always been better than a Movie. I was blessed to have lived a life close to a father like mine. This series of books, of which this is the second, is an attempt to share some of this life with my family and with you. My father was like a super hero, and together we never had a dull moment. I am older now, and feed off memories, so I decided to write a few down.

Chapter 13
WILD BOAR HUNTING AND TV TODAY

Television today has been good for most aspects of hunting. Through men like Bill Jordon of Realtree Camo, hunting shows on TV have been on the rise for 25 years or so. They have basically had a positive effect on the publics opinion of hunting. The makers of these shows show how the hunter helps thin the population of herds of deer for example, in areas where needed. They show how the planting of food plots for deer benefit hundreds of animals per each animal harvested. It shows the hunter in a conservation light, which of course he is. Not only is it the hunters dollars, through buying a hunting license, that pays for biologist to study the herds and set hunting regulations accordingly, but the hunter himself as an individual is concerned for the animal populations, so that he is insured something to hunt in years to come.

Your liberal groups like PETA, for example, say they love and care for animals but their rhetoric is primarily lip service and they never see the long term consequences of their actions. For example, they will raid a man's house and take his dogs because they do not think he is taking, what they consider to be, proper care of the animal. Then they send it to an animal shelter, where if it is not adopted in a certain time frame, it is put to death. Oh yeah, they make it sound nice, but they kill that man's dogs. A hunting example is the Semitar Horned Oryx. Texas hunting ranches brought the Oryx from over seas to introduce them to Texas as an animal to hunt. Now they are virtually extinct in the rest of the world. There are more Semitar Horned Oryx's in Texas today, than in the entire rest of the world combined. Texas Hunting Ranches saved the Oryx. No debate about it, they saved them. A few years back the World decided to put the Semitar Horned Oryx on the endangered species list, which would stop them from being hunted. Texas protested, because the only reason these hunting ranches are feeding all these Oryx's is to hunt. So uncommon on the world stage, before Donald Trump, the United States did the right thing. They said that the Oryx was an endangered species everywhere but the United States, and that's the way it stands today. The animal rights liberal groups flew into a rage. Then the US government explained that without Texas Hunters these animals would be extinct. Then one leading PETA lady said, "I would rather see them extinct than hunted". Yes you heard it correct. Typical liberal, they are not interested in what is best, just that the people they oppose do not get there way.

Another, more recent, liberal fiasco is now taking place with Lions in Africa. The majority of the Lions kept in Africa are kept by hunting ranches for hunters to harvest for money. After the American Dentist killed Cecil the Lion, the liberals had laws passed to stop the import of any Lion parts into the US. Well for African Hunting Ranches, the US hunters make up more than 85% of their customer base. When a hunter is not allowed to bring his Trophy home then he will not harvest it. That was the Liberal goal, but the consequences of there law was something different that they had planned. Not being able to hunt these Lions, the African lodges did not have a use for them. A thousand, or more, were simply put down. The only reason thousands more have not been put down, is in the hope that a sensible US President in the future will change the law. A similar fate happened with Elephants years ago. Again a liberal would rather see them killed than hunted. The killing of an Elephant in an African hunt, for example, is said to feed an African village for an average of 3 months. When an animal is hunted, then the hunter, and those who make a living off of hunters will take care of, and maintain hundreds of those animals just to harvest a chosen few.

The modern day hunting shows go to great lengths to point out such things. To show the hunter in the positive light he deserves. Bob Folkrod told me one time that many guys are wanting to make shows depicting what they call 'real hunting' where you wound the animal and chase him for mile, having to shoot him several more times to take him down. Sure this happens from time to time, but as Bob pointed out to me, the goal of these hunting shows for years now is not only to entertain hunters, but not to show the hunter as just a mindless barbarian killer. So for those wanting a 'reality hunting show', know that showing the barbaric side of it all may be fun for you at the time, but it is not in the best interest of hunters long term. These clean, ethical, shows help you with law makers. But these same ethical shows have had the opposite effect on Hog Hunters.

The little twist that these hunting shows have put on the hunting of hogs in North America has had a negative effect on Hog Hunting. These same shows that show Whitetail Deer hunting in a conservationist, what is best for the animal, light that promotes taking care of our nations Deer herds, take a different approach to Hogs. These shows portray hogs as evil demons out to destroy us all and the hunter as the savior of our nation. Hogs in the US today are portrayed in such a way that no one has to worry about the Russians, nor the Chinese, on the world stage because wild hogs are about to bust our doors down and kill us all. These modern TV shows call for the entire extermination of wild hogs. For example, I watched a show a while back where this guy starts the show in a panic stricken voice. He is standing in a cow pasture in Texas and yells for the camera to come look in a small creek on the Ranch. He says, "Mr. Johnson has lived on this cattle ranch his entire life. His family has owned this Ranch for 200 years. They are cattle farmers. They make a living and feed there small children with this cattle ranch. Now we realize that their entire lively hood is at risk. We have found Hog Feces in this creek. If we do not exterminate these hogs on this poor man's ranch, his entire family may be lost." Now for that idiots information there were hogs in Texas, brought to the Brownsville area by Hernando Desoto back in the 1500s, before there were cattle and white men. Hogs have been shitting in that same creek for the entire 200 years that that particular ranchers family has been building their cattle empire. You might say it was built on hog shit. The hogs on that particular ranch are no more disturbing the cattle there today than they were 100 years ago. But this is the way the modern day hunting TV shows choose to portray the hog. By doing this they give legitimacy to hunting. Now I am fine with painting a picture of hunting being a necessity, right up until it starts causing laws to be passed calling for the extermination of hogs in our country. See law makers nation wide have a tendency to watch these shows and actually believe what that little pip squick was saying about that poor cattle rancher and his, soon to be starving, family.

The truth is that I was raised in the deep south and spent my life in States that were saturated with hogs. We were still able to grow crops, go to the grocery store, attend school, and unless you were a hog hunter, hogs never crossed your mind. See many talk of the crop damage that hogs do nation wide. When in all actuality the crop damage done by Whitetail Deer nation wide far and away exceeds damage done by hogs. Many say that hogs compete with Deer for food. Well my experience from a life time of hog hunting all over the South Eastern portion of the United States is that in the places where we found the highest hog populations, we also found the highest Whitetail Deer populations. So if you are trying to insinuate that hogs hurt deer, you have my word that you are insane. Not only does my experience of a life time of hunting hogs and deer prove otherwise, but they seem to complement each other. If some hot shot Biologist would like to study my remarks, start in Jackson Alabama. You can't touch the ground in the swamp there without your finger on a hog, or deer, track. Both in equal numbers.

Proof that positions and law makers are taking these shows seriously and that it is effecting hog hunting laws can be found in the State of Tennessee. When I moved to Tennessee in 1995, hogs were treated as a game animal, just like Deer and Turkey. Hunting regulations protected Wild Boar. There were seasons on them, numbers of Boar that could be harvested, Sows and little ones were protected. Also the first Russians ever brought to the United States were brought to the Snowbird Mountain range right on the Tennessee - North Carolina border near Telico Tennessee. In around 1965 the Tennessee Wildlife Resources Agency, TWRA, started a trapping program to bring those Russians from the very Eastern parts of Tennessee to central Tennessee to a town called Crossville, in which can be found the Catoosa Wildlife Management area. This is one of, if not the, largest Wildlife Management Areas in the entire State of Tennessee. Yes, the State government of Tennessee itself spent almost 10 years spreading Wild Boar across the State. They were being spread, populated, and promoted as a large game animal by the State of Tennessee. Exactly like they spent years doing with Whitetail Deer and Eastern Wild Turkey. Then when these modern day hunting shows began, at some point enough Tennessee State Politicians began watching these shows and ordered a study done on the spread of the Evil Wild Boar across the State. The findings seemed to indicate from about 1964 until the present day of the study that hogs had seemed to explode from primarily Eastern Tennessee to central Tennessee. Well imagine that. What they failed to put in the report was that it was the State of Tennessee itself that was solely responsible for this spread. But this did not stop a series of laws coming down against hogs and hog hunters. No more is the hog considered a respected big game animal in the State, which they spent approximately 50 years promoting, he has now become, by all accounts, and 'Enemy of the State'. The laws concerning wild boar in the State of Tennessee seem to change every few weeks to deal with what these modern TV shows concerning hogs have caused Tennessee politicians to view as a State Emergency.

For a while the State of Tennessee's answer to the 'Hog Explosion' in the State was to stop the hunting of hogs all together. Yes you heard me right, hogs are everywhere according to the State, and to combat this we are going to stop hunters from killing them. Later I realized that it was a ploy to get Federal money. See the State of Kansas had pulled a stunt a few years earlier. A few hogs were quote "Reported' to be getting a foothold in the State. Due to this hog histeria caused solely by these modern TV shows, the State of Kansas was able to petition the Federal Government for a Million dollars to combat this situation. The first step Kansas had to take was to stop hunters from killing the hogs themselves. See any rational person seeing this situation would have simply opened a season on them and allowed the hunters of Kansas to handle the situation themselves. But governments have never been fond of the logical route. So Kansas outlawed the killing of these hogs by individual farmers, or hunters. This allowed them to beg for Federal Money. I was told by an unnamed USDA source that Kansas got, and spent a Million dollars of taxpayer money to hire government helecopter hunters to come in. That One Million dollars resulted in the killing of 53 hogs. Hunters could have done that in a weekend. So Tennessee proceeded with this first step to begging for Federal Government money by outlawing the hunting of wild hogs in the State. Well hunters went insane, threats were made, TWRA roads were tacked, game warden vehicles were vandalized, and 3 weeks later the State changed there stance on that attempt. Since then the law seems to change every year, but the change is always done in such a way as to lead to the extermination of one of the most resilient big game animals to ever grace the face of the Earth.

The Wild Boar, once hunted by Kings of every country across Europe, whose paintings are on European Cave Walls and also cover the canvases of European Art world wide, have been painted as demons that must be exterminated all due to Modern TV Hunting shows trying to justify the right to hunt to a bunch of liberals who claim to want what is best for all animals. These same liberals of course, who will die to save a spotted owl, but will violently attack you fighting to preserve a woman's right to kill her own unborn child. Tennessee, among other States, has now came up with another way to beg for Federal money by declaring it a war over the spread of disease. See the word disease seems to stimulate the giving of taxpayer dollars above all other things. These

States have zeroed in on the words Brucilousis and Pseudo Rabies. These are common things that many hogs carry. A completely different, unnamed, USDA source told me that every single wild hog tested in the State of Tennessee in 1972, tested positive for Brucilosis. The funniest thing about this 'Witch Hunt' for these two diseases is that they do not kill hogs, they just decrease pig production. Yes, again, you heard me right, in States that are in a full on panic mode about the, so called, explosion of hogs in their perspective States they want to combat a disease that would cause a decrease in pig production among Wild Hogs. Yes the insanity continues. They should be trying to promote the spread of such a disease, but instead that free taxpayer money that will keep them in a job sounds better.

States across the entire US have been on a similar attempt to beg for Taxpayers money to waste on another disease that is in the Whitetail Deer community. It is called CWD, or Chronic Wasting Disease. Each State petitions for money from the Feds every year to combat this and they spread mass hysteria among hunters about this and several related diseases. Now every one of these men who study these diseases have a degree, usually a PHD in Biology or Animal Husbandry. That means that each of them took Biology 101 in college. Even the most elementary Biology class teaches you the basics of wildlife. They teach that from time to time a disease, or an environmental pressure, will come along and hit a species of animal. It will kill a small percentage of them, but in the long run the result will be that the animals that have a natural resistance to that disease will survive and reproduce. The end result is a stronger, more disease resistant, heard of animals. So the smart thing to do is to allow Whitetail diseases like CWD and Blue Tongue to run its natural course, possibly even assist in the spread, and we will lose a certain percentage for a year or two, but in the end we will have a stronger nation wide herd of Whitetail Deer. That again, is Biology 101. But there is no Federal money in that for a State, so the mass hysteria begins. Taxpayer dollars spent hand over fist to stop something that is spread in the woods between wild animals and can never possibly be controlled. A small example of the State lunacy can be found in the North East. Many States are requiring hunters to turn in there deer kills for State testing for CWD. If they find your harvest to be positive for the disease, they want to know where it was taken, they then shut down hunting in that area, and bring in State paid hunters (with your taxpayers dollars) to exterminate all the deer in that area. Now what these geniuses are actually doing is going into an area where the disease has most likely killed the weak susceptible deer already, and they are destroying the healthy deer that have a natural immunity to the disease. They are killing the makings of that stronger herd previously discussed. State run lunacy, denying all their Biology 101 teachings, in the name of free money that makes them look good, because people are blind.

Wild hog populations in America are not on the rise, contrary to skewed studies created by States begging for Federal money. As a matter of fact it is just the opposite. I come from a long family of hog hunters. It began in Tennessee, where I can take you to farms who have always had an issue or two with hogs around planting time, just like they do with Whitetail Deer after growing of the crops start. These farmers will tell you that wild hogs have been in and around there farms for 5 generations of their family in this county. In the same county a mile away that farmer will tell you that they have never had hog issues for 5 generations. No spread of hogs you see, just hogs settled in areas where they have been for hundreds of years. My Daddy has hog hunted in Mississippi since I was born 50 years ago. When I was a little boy we had, let's say 50, places that we hunted regularly. Today hogs can be found in only around 10 of those places. I know hog hunters across the US, and the ones who are old and have seen the numbers from say the 1970s until today, will all tell you that the numbers are decreasing nation wide, except for in Texas. In Texas they stay the same. That is due to Texas having a 5,000 acre ranch here that allows hog hunting and then right next to it is a 10,000 acre ranch that does not want anyone hunting there. Hogs have safe havens in Texas. But the extermination policies caused by modern TV hunting programs will soon take effect there as well.

Hog hunters across the US have weathered this assassination barrage on this fine Trophy animal and have went along with it to some degree because they see it as loosening up laws on hogs and allowing them to hunt more, and be hailed as heroes to society. They have fell in with the TV stereotype and are happy to be viewed as doing a good service. But now they are starting to realize that painting their favorite game as 'public enemy number one' could turn to bite them in the butt. State lawmakers now started 'drinking the Koolaide' with these modern TV shows so much that many States are wanting to start, Federally Funded of course, programs to do mass poisoning on hogs across the US. So now an animal that was the top chosen among Kings to hunt, is now being treated like rodents. So wake up hog hunters across the US before your favorite big game animal to hunt is gone.

I believe that the Wild Boar should be treated with the respect he has earned as the most resilient of all big game animals. Hunters should treat him much the same as the Whitetail Deer or the Rocky Mountain Elk. Mature males should be harvested as the Trophies that they are, and the breed itself should be managed and maintained. This entire chapter is simply a product of Modern TV Shows starting out with good intentions of making the American Hunter appear to be doing a good service. Instead it should have been treating the Wild Boar as the same trophy animal as he portrays the Whitetail, and every other big game animal, on the same channel. Miss intended consequences.

Chapter 14
Spartan Hunting Preserve

After my father's death I began to formulate a plan. On our many visits to Crossville Tennessee as a young man we discovered a very interesting way to make a living. Crossville possessed two of the first ever "Hunting Preserves" for wild hog hunting. One was called Caryonah and the other was called Renegade Hunting Lodge. In it's very beginning my cousins Robert Kemmer and Johnny McCulloch both had worked for Renegade. On several occasions when we were in town we would take a ride out and visit both places. My Father, uncle Jack, and Grandfather would all talk about how very cool it would be to be able to make a living actually hunting hogs. They would all speak of it as an impossible dream, on scale of playing for the NFL. But I had lost my Grandfather in 1995 to a Heart Attack, then my father in 2000 to the same, so after the second loss I spent a great deal of time going over regrets. Along with these regrets I began to form a list of things that they had dreamed of. As the hog hunting lodge idea crossed my mind I settled on it. Now I loved my father and grandfather but they were not highly ambitious guys. There were neither ever late on a bill in their lives, but both viewed work as the enemy and only a way to buy groceries and fuel to go hunting and to other dog sports. But I on the other hand took after some of the extremely hard working women in my family like my Grandmothers on each side. Not being rich I knew that I would have to work hard at something my entire life, so what's the harm of hog hunting being that job.

I had started buying land in Tennessee at around 17 years old. My Grandfather owned some already, but I was a believer in land. Upon my arrival in Tennessee I continued to spend my money on land. I had a very successful Masonry Company rolling at the point that my father passed, but I soon began the plans and steps to beginning a Wild Boar Hunting Lodge. Checking with the TWRA to find out the rules, it all began to take shape. One of my children told my mother what I had been thinking about. My mother paid me the finest compliment I could ever receive by saying, "Well if your father says he is going to open a Hunting Lodge, then he will open a Hunting Lodge". I began to speak to other lodge owners about the steps involved. One lodge owner named Matt Shoats told me that it would be the coolest thing in the world to have a Hog Hunting Lodge that was actually ran by a Hog Hunter. See earlier that year Matt had been approached by a TV show about a hog hunting episode that they had planned. They assumed that since he ran a hog hunting preserve, that he was actually a hog hunter. It is a common misconception, but as they approached him he quickly pointed out their error and had them call me. It is a man of character who can admit the truth.

My wife's first question was how I expected to make it in a business that already had so many competitors in our particular area. Our area was covered with 6 or 8 lodges due to folks working at Caryonah when they were high school kids, liking the idea, and starting their own. But when the question was poised to me by her my answer was that I planned to use the same unusual business maneuver that I had used to make my Brick Masonry Company so successful. I told her, "I am going to do exactly what I say, exactly when I say it". Honesty and honor, what a bold concept.

I then began collecting hogs to begin the breeding programs for what I wanted. I went through all the channels with the USDA that the TWRA had prescribed. I also began my fencing. Yes preserves are fenced, just like every place you hunt in South Africa or New Zealand. See with the hog hysteria caused by modern hunting shows on TV, the only way the State of Tennessee will allow you to deal with a hog is on an extermination policy. In Tennessee if you accidentally catch a hog in a trap, it is illegal to turn him loose alive. So if I ran a hunting lodge free range in Tennessee then it would have to be operated on the same extermination policy that Texas uses, which to me is disgusting. The animal himself is treated with no respect at all. The finest Big Game animal on the continent, once the favorite hunted animal by kings and royalty, and now their babies are exterminated like roaches. If Texas treated their deer population the way they treat their hog population, you would never kill a trophy. The State of Tennessee orders us to do the same thing if we free range hunt. I wanted to treat the Wild Boar like the respected Trophy Animal that he is. So fenced preserves were the plan. Simply fence a large area in the Mountains of East Tennessee, just like I have seen in Africa, New Zealand, and most of Texas for that matter. Then I would fill it with the finest stock the continent had to offer, allow them to breed and reproduce totally wild in these areas for at least 5 years before opening to the public, and then selectively hunt for Trophies from that established population.

I then began working towards that very goal with every extra dime I had from my Masonry job. I was working 7 days a week at times to achieve this goal. My research had shown me that there were five lines of Russians, or Europeans, in North America, the Kalden, the Andreas, the Bzikot, the San Diego line (brought in by the San Diego Zoo), and of course the old original Russians still populating all of East, and central TN due to the TWRA. So I began my collection having the Tennessee USDA blood test all the original stock to check for the silly diseases that they seem to think important. I also began to look at Desoto Feral lines as well. Being an actual hog hunter, and knowing of strange lines of hogs such as Wattle Hogs, Mule Footed Hogs, and the ever illusive Possum Blue hog, I wanted to have the genetics for them all. I did not want even the most seasoned hog hunter to call me and ask for something that I did not have the potential to have. Taking them all through the health channels, we got our areas fenced and began our breeding program to produce Trophies for our future. After a little over 5 years of establishing a fine population of Wild Boar, we opened our doors to the public in February of 2008. After that I gradually weened from the Brick Job to the Hunting Lodge as business picked up.

Upon a hunters arrival at the lodge I always insisted on giving them "the Speech". This is an orientation designed to give them a brief education on hogs. I have often hunted at places where I was just cast into the woods with no info nor personal attention. The speech, designed by me, is meant to educate them on the variety of hogs that they are about to encounter. The goal of the hunt is to insure that they get the trophy that they want. See there are basically 3 types of hogs. Europeans, of which there are 5 lines, and we are the only hunting lodge in the entire country that have all 5. Color, tail length, size to some degree, can tell one the differences in these 5 lines. Also there are 2 types of Feral Boars, one is the Desoto line that I had hunted my entire life, and the other is a much bigger hog with genetics in him that are closer to what we would think of as domestic today. Now the Russians and the Desoto Feral Boars all top out at somewhere between 300 to 350 pounds, occasionally one might hit the 400 mark. But this other type of Feral is like the Hogzilla Boar killed years ago. He is a Boar that may reach the 600 to 800 pound range due to the fact that he is closely related to the Domestic Boar of today which has been bred for hundreds of years for this large size. Now he can be totally wild like the Hogzilla Boar, or like the 500 pound sow from McNeil that paralyzed Baby Boy, but this monster size is the give away of his genetics. An example of why I like to give the speech is to describe such facts, because if a person saw one of these 600 pounders walk by their stand, they might say, "Well that is the size I want, and when I see a Russian that size I will take him". Well after the speech they know a Russian can not get to that size. Preparation for the hunt can save mistakes in the woods.

Now other lodges just allow people to go amble about on there own to hunt. I have learned that hunting out of Stands is much safer and is very successful. We put folks in stands and do not allow them to leave the stand without a guide. When I place someone in a stand, I tell them they can shoot in any direction they like without fear of hitting another hunter. Then me and my crew begin scouting for hogs. This serves to either spook a hog towards a stand, or we may spot a good one bedded some where, go to the stand and get the hunter, and proceed with a guided spot and stalk all of the time with the goal to take only big mature boars.

Now I was raised hog hunting with dogs, but noticed all my life that we only caught on average about two real Trophy Boars a year after the stock law days in the beginning. Dogs do not discriminate and more often than not end up on a small hog or a sow who does not have the experience to clear out. It is crucial to me that we very selectively Trophy Hunt. So dog hunting was out. Also many ask me about night hunting to which I give the same reasoning. It is hard to judge size, shape, color, distance, etc., at night so a selective hunt for a nice Trophy is almost impossible with a light or night vision. Leave that to the extermination States, with no Trophy aspirations. Also I won't even go into that "STAGED" Helicopter Hunting. No, stand hunting and a good spot and stalk is the best way to Trophy Hunt.

Many of my friends ask me how I have resigned myself to guiding hunts after leading such an exciting life of adrenaline filled action. My answer is that I am making a living doing what I love to do. I also point out the challenge of taking a hunter and getting him on a specific Trophy, and the pleasure that can bring. It is a way of promoting the Trophy hunting of an animal that is being completely misrepresented and misunderstood in our country today. I tell people that if you want to go 'plinking' go to Wyoming and shoot ground hogs, but when it comes to the Wild Boar, treat him with the respect he has earned.

This change in attitudes about the Wild Boar can be contributed to more than just modern hunting TV shows trying to paint another reason to justify hunting to a pansy section of the country. The State of Florida gives us another reason. It sees an influx of yankees, most of whom are not hunters, nor have many of them ever been around wildlife of any kind. They arrive with a condescending attitude of Southerners, and all things Southern. They arrive with the attitude that not only have they come to change us, but to save us from ourselves. Now mind you I am not talking about Northern Hunters, anyone who hunts is what I call a person that is 'in touch with reality'. I am talking about that liberal group of Yankees that, typical of liberals everywhere, believe that if they don't believe in it, then it has to be wrong. It is these type of people who move to Florida, buy a house in the middle of an ole Okachobie Swamp, backed up to the edge of a slue full of Alligators, then golf on a course that was also built in that same swamp where Wild Boar have been since released by Hernando Desoto in 1539. Then each time a lizard or a snake shows up on their back deck, they quickly call for animal control and cause a scene worthy of a reality show. Any true Southerner still in Florida that has a Gator hanging around his back yard trying to ambush his pet, he simply shoots the Gator, chops off his tail, throws it on the grill, and kicks the Gator back into the slue to become fish food, and no one is the wiser. But it is these jumpy liberal intruders into what was the hogs home just a few years ago that calls the Game Commission every time a hog roots up the corner of his yard, or a portion of that golf course. So then a State that used to be full of Southerners who took care of things themselves, has suddenly turned into a State that sees officials and representatives receiving cry baby phone calls about the evil wild hogs. So instead of the State itself taking into consideration what the State population has turned into, choose to fall in with the modern hunting shows they too have been watching and believe that hog populations in Florida are on the rise. Talk to any old hog hunter from the 70s, that has a rational mind that is, and he will tell you there is no increase.

Another fault lies with actual hunters themselves, related to this new dim view of the wild boar. In the last 20 to 30 years a new craze has hit the hunting community. That is the "Food Plot" phase. Now food plots and automatic feeders are a wonderful thing and feed hundreds of animals, per each animal taken. I love food plots and agree whole heartedly that they benefit wildlife enormously. But you go deep into a swamp, the only place a Wild Boar has left on this continent to exist, and you clear a spot and plant some nice green tasty Rye Grass, maybe even put up a feeder slinging out whole corn every day. Now process that in your mind for a second. So that Wild Boar that lived peacefully in that Swamp in 1980, who you rarely ever saw, or noticed, on your deer hunt, now is pissing you off because he has, as a part of the Wildlife, took part in your Wildlife Feeding Gallery that you put right in his living room. So the hog that you never noticed before the age of Food Plots, you now notice, so you choose to think that the numbers of them are increasing like the TV show you watch at supper every night says.

Then there is the the 'ever so popular' people in States that are imagining that they have Wild Boar. When the TV hype about this first started every little armadillo scratching turned into hog sign. I run a hunting lodge now where I talk to people from many Northern States that have a wild imagination, just like many Southerners do with Armadillo sign, and they are going on Rumors. We get a lot of hunters from Indiana for example, and for years everyone who has ever shown up at my place relays to me the fact that, "We are starting to get them in the Southern part of our State". Which of course seems very strange to me because the State of Kentucky has never had hog problems, so I usually don't assume they jumped a whole State. So I asked every Indianian, "Have you ever seen one?", or "Do you know anyone who has seen one?", and of course the answer is always no. I get this same thing from Virginia, Maryland, and even New York State. I have come to believe that it is a panic caused by the ever so popular Hunting Shows, or in some cases a farmer had a weak fence in isolated incidences and a few tame hogs got out. The 'Pot Belly Pig' craze a few years ago, saw many pet owners turning out their swine companions here and there across the nation, but a lone pig here and there does not constitute them getting a foothold in a State. But the point is that the 'Hog Hysteria' caused by the TV has caused imaginations to run wild nation wide. So instead of seeing this Trophy Animal as the ultimate challenge for a hunter that he has been viewed since the beginning of time, we have gotten into a panic mode at his very mention.

Now through a lifetime of hunting with my grandfather I experienced hunting every animal that the deep South had to offer. Upon reaching adulthood I began going out West and to Canada to hunt other Big Game Species that North America had to offer. Then in later life was finally able to achieve a lifelong dream of hunting both

Africa and New Zealand. Like many hunters this helped me to develop a deep respect for each animal that I have pursued. This material that I have presented to you here, however, is given to try and convey to each of you the deep respect for an animal that has always been my favorite, and most respected adversary to pursue. I wanted to share many stories of pursuit in an attempt to help you develop a sense of his courage, intelligence, evasiveness, and toughness, in a hope that you will begin to see him as I always have, and in the way that Kings and Queens of old viewed him. If you chose not to view him as the single most challenging and rewarding hunt on the planet, as my father did, then at least put him back in his long held place among the top Big Game Trophies in the World.

As for my life of being raised a hog hunter, I wouldn't trade it for anything. The United States is full of hunters. Owning a hunting lodge today puts me in contact with hunters from coast to coast, and I have found that their are fine people in every State of the Union that share this passion. Hunting to me should be in a person's nature. We are the number one predator on the planet and at whatever age you begin hunting, to me you should take to it like a fish to water. Being raised in South Mississippi every young man where I was from was born into hunting and I was lucky enough to be born into a family that hunting was ingrained into. I have friends who may hunt everything but who live to hunt Turkey, other's who love to Bear hunt, and other's still who love Whitetail Deer. My Grandfather indoctrinated me into every kind of hunting our area provided, later in life I sought out other big game around the world, but my father was a dog man and a hog hunter. He combined the two and it became a passion for him. Looking back on it all, Hog Hunting was always my favorite. Much like my father a Big Mature Wild Boar is what always tripped my trigger. I have to agree with Kings of old, that he is the most worthy advisory for me. If I were King and had to design my Medal of Honor, I would have to agree with King Richard III of England, a King that chose to die in a full on charge against overwhelming enemy forces. I think I would have chosen the Wild Boar to represent me as well. My father's own death of a heart attack while hog hunting resembled the death of France's King Philip IV. When the Wild Boar charged Philip's horse and he fell from it, it was a massive stroke that actually killed him. Tough men going after tough animals. My Grandfather, uncle, and father were all tough men. The American Pit Bull Terrier has the toughness and gameness that I respect above all other things, and the Wild Boar provides me with the best challenge any big game animal could offer because he possesses those same traits.

Tough men, tough dogs, going after the toughest big game animal on their continent. All in all Hog Hunting just seemed to fit my nature.

I had a German tell me one time that the United States was the finest country in the world for hunters. He said in all the other countries in the world, that only the wealthy were legally allowed to hunt. In the old days only Kings and Noblemen hunted. In Germany and around the world today, other than the US, only people with money can hunt. As I was flying into New Zealand in the summer of 2018 to take all the Big Game animals that that country had to offer, I had to take a plane from the North Island to the South Island. On that flight I was seated near a New Zealander who was a hunter. I began asking him if he had ever killed certain animals that I was there to take. He answered that all he could ever afford to hunt was rabbits. The Red Stag, Tahr, Chamois, and Fallow Deer were only for people with money to hunt. When I was in Africa in the summer of 2016, I was definitely aware that hunting was only for the wealthy on that continent. So the old German was correct and I had never thought of it. In the United States, with the purchase of a simple inexpensive hunting license, every man is given the right to hunt. What a lucky man I was to be born into such a fine country.

The United States today, however, has became a country that does not respect the same things in life that I was raised to respect. I have always been raised to respect toughness and gameness. Now in our beginning the United States loved and respected Warrior's like George Washington, Alexander Hamilton, and Andrew Jackson. But the America I see today not only looks down on truly tough men. The America that I see today seems to celebrate weakness in men. Any thing that tough men, especially tough white men, do seems to be demonized. When a country stops respecting the tough men that that same country depends on to protect them from their enemies, something is wrong. So wrong that those same people seem to get confused as to which bathroom to use. It then becomes a country where it is okay to "Self Identify" as a man or a woman. The United States today says that if you wake up and decide to be one gender, or the other, you may choose day by day. A few years back, for example, a man power lifter woke up one morning and decided that that day he felt like he was a woman. So he went and joined a woman's power lifting meet, and although he had a penis, he now holds several women's power lifting records.

So taking this sort of lunatic rational into consideration it makes it easier for me to understand this recent shift in Americas attitude towards the Wild Boar. The Wild

Boar went from being painted on cave walls to being literally a Big Game Animal whose pursuit was a Sport of Kings. Today throughout the continent of Europe the hunting of the Wild Boar is still one of the most time honored traditions of all hunting sports. Hernando Desoto dropped the first Wild Boar here because his toughness made him the only animal that explorers could count on to survive anywhere along their travels. Once colonization started it was the Boar that could be released in the woods and counted on to survive, reproduce successfully in the woods, and become a main staple in the diets of farmers. Being able to rely on this animals heartiness made it where poor farmers could have large numbers of hogs without having to financially support them with feed. After stock laws were passed State by State, the Wild Boar again became an animal for hunters to pursue. States like Tennessee put them under strict game laws, and the State itself, trapped and transported them across the State of Tennessee. All of this done with respect of the animal and in an attempt to promote him as the fine Big Game Trophy animal that Kings had always viewed him as. Dog Hunters across the Deep South began viewing him as the finest competition on this continent to pursue. Then came the dreaded modern TV hunting shows, who decided to paint him as a nuisance animal just to appease the left wing side of the country. These left wing people who do not know which bathroom to use, or do not know whether they are a man or a woman, view all hunting as evil. It falls into their view that anything done by primarily White Men has to be evil. So the modern TV shows are trying to appease them by saying that the killing of a Wild Boar, is a "necessary evil". To successfully paint this picture they have went to great extremes to paint the Wild Boar as a destructive nuisance that must be hunted in an extermination fashion, and the silly hunting community has bought in. Now wild hogs are destroyed on site from the day they are born and even babies are slaughtered wholesale. What you people need to come to grips with is that you will never satisfy the left. They not only want to destroy everything that you do, but they want to destroy you as well. Their appetite can never be satisfied.

The United States is headed in a direction that I can never agree with, but I have never seen it more evident than in the way they have chosen to view the single finest Big Game Animal that has ever graced their continent. Cave men viewed the Wild Boar as one of their most challenging pursuits. Kings Viewed him as the single finest challenging hunt that they could take. He was viewed as so tough that he tested the courage of kings. Deer, or stag, hunting was always viewed as a fun hunt, but not a challenge of courage. Wild Boar hunting was used world wide as a test for military men from India to Northern England. The hunting of Wild Boar was told as the biggest challenges for even the Mythological Hero's told in stories of old. The toughest tribes of Africa saw the killing of a Lion as a passage into manhood for their future leaders of their tribes. But from Northern England to Southern Spain, from France to the coldest Siberian parts of Russia and stretching down into India, it was the hunting of a Wild Boar that was viewed as the 'right to passage' into manhood. In the United States beginning they showed this animal the respect he deserved as a Warrior, just as they showed George Washington and Andrew Jackson the respect they deserved as warriors. But this US drift to the left that demonizes tough men, has also began to demonize the single finest Big Game Animal to ever grace this continent. What a shame.

This photo was published in an Outdoor Magazine put out in Central and East Tennessee. I went up to visit my Grandfather at the same time that my cousin David Mitchell happened to be there, so we all struck out on a hog hunt one morning and bagged this fine Russian. From left to right is Edward Garring, Charlie Kemmer, David Mitchell, David Nelson, Leko Kemmer, and Mitch Kemmer.

From my birth I have enjoyed the pursuit of this fine animal. My father chose to hunt him with dogs in the same fashion that he was once hunted by Kings. Norman Kemmer respected a good tough mature Wild Hog, like the Red Gap Boar, as much as he respected anything or anyone. I was raised to admire the Wild Boar in the very same fashion. After my father's death I started my hunting lodge in an attempt to bring some semblance of respect back to the pursuit of this animal. All Texas and Florida lodges that hunt this animal do it on the new TV extermination policy. Lodges in my area who do not necessarily hunt on a 'plinking style' extermination policy, still harvest their animals too young. By killing a Boar before he has reached the maturity age of 3 to 5 years old, you are taking an animal before his teeth have even developed. It would be like taking a Whitetail Deer as a spike or a four point. Now that's better than taking him with the spots still on him, which is the equivalency of what hog hunting in Texas and Florida is today, but it is still not maturity. If you ever speak to me for more than 5 minutes on the subject of hog hunting you will quickly see my respect for this Royal and Regal Trophy. If you ever hunt with me it will be in a manner that gives this animal the respect he deserves, by only trying to take mature trophies.

My family has encouraged me for years to write down some of the chapters of my life. This book is an attempt to cover the widest chapter of them all and that is my life concerning the Wild Boar. I come from a family of dog men. My Grandfather and then my father both never spent a day in their lives without contact with a dog. My father's life in the dogs took him in two directions. I was blessed to be allowed to enjoy them both, but one of them made me a hog hunter. That passion was the one that eat me up the most as a young boy, and in the end has been the one that has followed me for the whole of my life. Like King Richard III, like the military 'lancers' from India, and like Norman Kemmer, I believe that there is no finer Trophy that lives on this planet than a Mature Wild Boar. The animal that can drink at a water hole between two Tigers. The animal that King Philip IV and Norman Kemmer took their deaths in pursuit of. A Trophy Animal that deserves the utmost admiration.

This is a strain of Pure Russian, that can be found on our Hunting Preserve today. There is no Big Game Trophy finer than a good Wild Boar.

www.ingramcontent.com/pod-product-compliance
Lightning Source LLC
Chambersburg PA
CBHW042016090426
42811CB00015B/1656
* 9 7 8 1 7 3 2 8 2 8 3 1 5 *